Preparing Change Agents for the Classroom

From Paradigm to Practice

Jill E. Cole

ROWMAN & LITTLEFIELD EDUCATION
A division of
ROWMAN & LITTLEFIELD PUBLISHERS, INC.
Lanham • New York • Toronto • Plymouth, UK

Published by Rowman & Littlefield Education
A division of Rowman & Littlefield Publishers, Inc.
A wholly owned subsidiary of The Rowman & Littlefield Publishing Group, Inc.
4501 Forbes Boulevard, Suite 200, Lanham, Maryland 20706
http://www.rowmaneducation.com

Estover Road, Plymouth PL6 7PY, United Kingdom

Copyright © 2012 by Jill E. Cole

All rights reserved. No part of this book may be reproduced in any form or by any electronic or mechanical means, including information storage and retrieval systems, without written permission from the publisher, except by a reviewer who may quote passages in a review.

British Library Cataloguing in Publication Information Available

Library of Congress Cataloging-in-Publication Data

Cole, Jill E., 1956-
Preparing change agents for the classroom : how teachers can make a difference in learning / Jill E. Cole.
p. cm.
Includes bibliographical references and index.
ISBN 978-1-61048-053-6 (hardback) -- ISBN 978-1-61048-054-3 (paper) -- ISBN 978-1-61048-055-0 (electronic)
1. Teachers--Training of. 2. Constructivism (Education) 3. Learning strategies. I. Title.
LB1707.C64 2012
370.71'1--dc23

2011046714

The paper used in this publication meets the minimum requirements of American National Standard for Information Sciences Permanence of Paper for Printed Library Materials, ANSI/NISO Z39.48-1992.

Printed in the United States of America

To Tom, my loving husband and editorial assistant extraordinaire.

Contents

Acknowledgments   vii

Introduction   ix

1   Preparing Change Agents for the Classroom Using the Constructivist Paradigm   1
Jill E. Cole

Turning Point: From Preservice to Inservice   5
Kristin Thompson, 2nd/3rd Grade Teacher

2   Beyond the Algorithm: Changing Teacher Candidates' Learning Experiences with Mathematics   9
B. Patricia Patterson

Turning Point: Lost and Found   31
Jamie Whitman-Smithe, Teacher Educator

3   Writing Workshop for Teacher Candidates   33
Jill E. Cole

Turning Point: The Spelling Test   51
Paula P. Daniels, First-Grade Teacher

4   Crafting Inquiry in the Preservice Classroom: Tensions and Possibilities   53
Leah T. Lembo

Turning Point: Change of Plans   73
Patti L. Sandy, 1st Grade Teacher

5	Changing Preservice Teachers' Perceptions of Science and Science Teaching through Guided Nature Journaling *B. Patricia Patterson*	75
	Turning Point: Leaf Collecting *Ivey Mask, Graduate Student, Journal Entry*	95
6	Story in the Classroom *Jamie Whitman-Smithe*	97
	Turning Point: Teaching Molly *Megan Stoffa, Teacher Candidate*	111
7	Helping Teacher Candidates Develop the Skills of Reflective Practitioners *Marcia P. Lawton*	113
Closing		127
Contributors		129

Acknowledgments

First, I would like to thank all the contributing authors for sharing their content expertise and their passion for teaching. Everyone was so generous with their time: sharing stories, discussing chapters, writing drafts, revising, and preparing the final manuscript. It was a journey I was privileged to share with these colleagues and friends.

Thanks also goes to those who took the time and energy to read and give feedback on the manuscript. Dr. Pam Farris and Carol McCullough provided insights which made such a difference in the finished book.

Finally, I want to express my appreciation to Dr. Tom Koerner, vice president and editorial director, for his support and encouragement during this process. He and Lindsey Schauer, assistant editor, were always quick to respond to my many emailed questions. Thank you.

Introduction

What Is a Change Agent?

Consider the following situations, the risks being taken, the educational impact, and the potential rewards for the students and teachers.

Mr. Murphy and his colleagues conduct action research in their classrooms to look at the effectiveness of their current social studies program. The results are disappointing. They meet with the principal and discuss replacing the social studies textbook with one they feel focuses on "big" questions that students care about rather than names and dates.

Mrs. Whitman purchases math manipulatives to augment her mathematics program even though no one else on the fifth-grade team elects to do the same. She reads professional literature to inform her use of the manipulatives in her classroom.

After studying award-winning young adolescent literature, Ms. Esteban orders paperback books for her middle schoolers who refuse to read the selections in the reading textbook.

Mr. Chen is passionate about science but he notices his students are not. He attends a science conference to learn strategies for teaching student-generated inquiry projects.

Ms. Martinez is frustrated by the district policy for identifying students who struggle with academics. She feels the policy only benefits students with significant need and should be changed to provide help for other struggling learners. She attends a school board meeting to express her concern.

These teachers are change agents. They have made the decision to go the extra mile to meet the learning needs of their students. They are willing to bring about educational reform, which can mean anything from curriculum changes in a social studies program to policy changes at the state Department of Education. A change agent may reorganize, recast, transform, initiate, trigger, or even revolutionize. No change is too small or too large for it to affect the meaning of a child's experience in school.

We need change agents in our classrooms right now. The purpose of this book is to describe philosophy and teaching strategies for the college/university classroom that can inspire change agency in our teacher candidates. If you are attempting to mold your teacher candidates into those who make a difference in the field of education, this book is for you.

We believe that one way to embolden change agency in our candidates is to equip them with constructivist strategies such as the ones described in this book. These are not new methods – constructivism has been supported in the literature and successfully used in classrooms for decades. While implementing the methods involves some risk and trust, there is nothing quite as satisfying as influencing a student who becomes a learner for life. The chapters in the book are written by teacher educators who use constructivist strategies in the college/university classroom to support teacher candidates who are learning what it means to be a teacher for positive change.

The book begins with a description of the constructivist paradigm as it will be used by the authors. It provides a foundation for the rest of the chapters which address constructivist teaching in each content area: math, science, social studies, and language arts.

Between each chapter in the book is a *Turning Point* – less academic and more heartfelt accounts of teaching and learning. In the first *Turning Point*, Kristin Thompson shares her experience of becoming a constructivist learner in college and then a constructivist teacher in her own classroom. While it is essential to look at effective, constructivist teaching strategies, the *Turning Points* capture the passion of constructivist teaching and learning that results in change. These intimate portraits are presented to encourage you with real-life stories of success and to remind you to take notice of the turning points in your own students as they learn and grow.

The following chapters explain specific strategies that can be used to promote constructivist teaching in the classroom and to develop a spirit of change agency in our teacher candidates. In chapter two, B. Patricia Patterson takes you *Beyond the Algorithm* as she describes how to teach math so candidates understand the concepts behind the numbers and learn the skills to teach those concepts in their own classrooms. In a later chapter, she demonstrates how nature journals engage candidates to look at and teach about our earth in a new way.

Jill Cole lays out a framework for a motivational college-level writing workshop that can easily be re-created in the elementary or secondary classroom. The effective use of inquiry in science and social studies is explained by Leah Lembo. Jamie Whitman-Smithe discusses the value of story in all of our teaching, and Marcia Lawton closes the book by providing ideas on how we can encourage candidates to be reflective practitioners, which often leads to important change.

Preparing change agents for the classroom is a job that the authors of this book take seriously but also with joy. What an honor it is to make a difference in the lives of students in grades K-12 through their teachers. Each chapter, and each *Turning Point,* in this book reflects a unique voice to share philosophy, strategies, and change for the classroom. May the voices resonate with your own.

Chapter One

Preparing Change Agents for the Classroom Using the Constructivist Paradigm

Jill E. Cole

A change agent is someone who changes the meaning of a child's experience (Dewey, 1913; Gowin, 1981). Constructivists accomplish this change by helping students connect new knowledge to their existing knowledge, resulting in learning.

A change agent says, "I'm going to teach the way children learn" and acquires a toolkit of strategies to carry it out in the classroom. Constructivist-based strategies provide a foundation for meaningful, important curriculum that teachers can use to be change agents in their classrooms. Teacher candidates who experience constructivist teaching and learning in the college/university classroom will be equipped with the skill to develop and use the strategies needed to become change agents for their students.

The authors of this book define constructivism as a philosophical paradigm. A philosophy is "a system of values by which one lives" (American Heritage College Dictionary, 2004, p. 1045) and a paradigm is a "pattern or model" (American Heritage College Dictionary, 2004, p. 1008) for those values, concepts, and practices. It is impossible to simply "do" constructivism, an educator must "be" a constructivist.

The constructivist philosophy is not about how we should teach, but about how human beings learn. It maintains that we learn by constructing new knowledge through connections to current knowledge structures and experiences. Learning, then, is a process of adjusting existing understandings to accommodate new experiences.

This is in opposition to the notion that our students are empty vessels waiting to "be filled with information" through lectures and memorization of facts. Constructivist educators strive to teach not only to content standards but also to students' needs and interests, using appropriate instructional models. Constructivism emerged from learning philosophy *and* classroom-based research, making it a compelling model for use in the classroom.

Cognitive constructivism and social constructivism are two branches of the philosophical paradigm. Cognitive constructivism focuses on the learner as an individual. Prior knowledge, experiences, beliefs, and values influence how a learner perceives new information (Piaget, 1970). Social constructivism includes the learner's construction of knowledge through social interactions (Vygotsky, 1962).

Learning involves cognitive and social components, both of which are necessary for meaningful learning. Therefore, some educators have suggested a merging of cognitive and social constructivist perspectives, maintaining that knowledge is personally constructed as well as socially mediated (Moore, 2004). This melding of perspectives is the stance taken by the authors of this book and is referred to by the term "constructivist" and exemplified by the methods and strategies described in the following chapters.

Constructivists believe the following about the classroom experience (Brooks & Brooks, 2001):

- Learners need developmentally appropriate instruction so they can construct their own knowledge. Their opinions and questions are valued and integral to the process.
- Instructors facilitate meaning construction by seeking students' current perceptions before planning appropriate lessons. They pose important questions and encourage conversation, risk-taking, and connections to real life.
- The curriculum includes multiple resources, such as primary sources, manipulatives, and technology and is presented from whole to part with emphasis on big concepts.
- Instructors and students set collaborative goals for learning as well as for behaviors in the classroom.
- Assessment of student work (formative and summative) is interwoven with teaching.

However, these beliefs are only as strong as the classroom practices that exemplify them. For example, teacher educators may begin a course on constructivist practices with a discussion of candidate's previous experiences with school before introducing writing workshop, student-generated inquiry, or concept mapping. The teacher educator knows that he needs to connect his candidate's prior experiences to the constructivist strategies he will soon be teaching. As the class works together, the instructor guides a continual refinement of content and strategies that will equip teacher candidates with the knowledge, skills, and dispositions to teach with passion and confidence.

Knowing that the philosophical beliefs we hold shape our practice, we strive to hold true to the constructivist paradigm and act as change agents for our teacher candidates. We believe that, in turn, the teacher candidates will learn how to be change agents for their own students, creating motivated learners who will continue to learn throughout their lives.

REFERENCES

American Heritage College Dictionary (2004). (4th ed.). Boston: Houghton Mifflin.
Brooks, J.G., & Brooks M.G. (2001) *The case for constructivist classrooms.* Upper Saddle River, NJ: Prentice-Hall.
Dewey, J. (1913). *Interest and effort in education.* Boston: Riverside.
Gowin, D.B. (1981). *Educating.* Ithaca, NY: Cornell University Press.
Moore, W.S. (2004). Understanding learning in a postmodern world: Reconsidering the Perry scheme of ethical and intellectual development. In B.K. Hofer & P.R. Pintrich (Eds.), *Personal epistemology* (pp. 17-36). Mahwah, NJ: Erlbaum.
Piaget, J. (1970). *The science of education and the psychology of the child.* New York: Orion Press.
Vygotsky, L. (1962). *Thought and language.* Cambridge: MIT Press.

Turning Point: From Preservice to Inservice

Kristin Thompson, 2nd/3rd Grade Teacher

It was freshman orientation in college. All of the teacher candidates were instructed to meet in a large room. I was surprised to see such a high proportion of our student body filling the conference room to capacity with eager teacher hopefuls. After a few informational tidbits, a professor instructed us to look to our left, and then to our right. She proceeded to announce that two out of the three of us would not be graduating as teachers. The room echoed with giggles, probably all thinking the same as me, "It can't really be that hard."

On my graduation day, I didn't see those students who had been on my left and on my right. I celebrated with only 12 fellow classmates. The professor had been right; it was that hard.

For me and many of my classmates, the journey to becoming a constructivist teacher was a frustrating yet amazing experience.

In college I was taught to teach the way children learn using the constructivist philosophy. But this mode of learning and teaching was difficult for me to accept because it was so different from the way I had been educated. In most of my elementary and high school classes, I was expected to absorb information and facts by listening to lectures, taking notes, and then regurgitating the lists and names and dates on tests to prove that I was being educated.

In college I found learning constructivist concepts daunting because they required deep, critical thinking. We weren't being spoon-fed information, we were changing the way we thought and the way we learned. We were expected to question the content and search out new answers, set personal learning goals and self-evaluate, become self-directed learners and observant student teachers.

I have since learned that being educated as a constructivist teacher just begins the process, and that becoming a skilled constructivist teacher is a lifetime endeavor...but I didn't realize that when I started teaching in my own classroom.

When the school year began and the students actually arrived in my classroom, my theoretical knowledge quickly began to search for quick, practical solutions to the problems I encountered. It was easy to fall back on a non-constructive approach. It wasn't news to me that students enter the classroom with a wide range of experiences and come from varied socioeconomic backgrounds, cultures, and medical histories. The thing that hadn't sunk in yet was that even the best-prepared lesson plans cannot be a one-size-fits-all. Neither can a single approach to classroom management. Students are diverse.

If I've had a turning point on my constructivist journey, it was in dealing with a child who was a problem that very first day of teaching in my own classroom.

The student became enraged when I asked him to talk with me for a few minutes about taking another student's school supply box. He threw chairs and yelled foul words before storming out of the classroom and into the boys' bathroom.

This behavior continued for many weeks. I attempted to punish this behavior, threaten (and follow through), alert his parents after each incident, and reward with candy when desired behaviors were performed. It soon became obvious my initial plan was not working.

After a couple of months, I was mentally worn out. I decided one day to take a few minutes to have a one-on-one conversation with the boy. The more I spoke with him, the more I learned. He came from a low income home; he feared his father; his parents were rarely home due to work schedules. No one was reading to him at home or helping with homework. I began to understand this child's behavior, and I knew I needed to change the meaning of school and learning for this boy.

This boy needed a safe place, and our classroom became his comfort zone. External motivators didn't work, so I directed my attention to building a strong relationship with him. When he became enraged, I did not respond by yelling, punishing, or threatening. Rather, I calmly would ask him, "What do you need?"

Over time, the boy learned he did not have to act abusive or infuriated to get my attention. We developed a relationship where he felt comfortable enough to approach me with his needs and wants, both personal and academic. He read the books I selected with his interests in mind. He completed his math when I explained why it was important. He became interested in science inquiry when he could do further research and share his discoveries with his classmates.

Consequently, behavior issues diminished drastically and his learning progressed at a slow, but steady rate. Although an investment of time was required, the mutual respect we built for each other made all the difference. The process was tough but we both had a firmer foundation on which to build our educational journey.

When I entered a constructivist teacher education program, it was overwhelming. When I started teaching in my own classroom, it was challenging. When I had to deal with the students who struggled, it was exhausting. But when those students began to demonstrate that they were becoming successful learners - oh, how sweet were those turning points.

Chapter Two

Beyond the Algorithm: Changing Teacher Candidates' Learning Experiences with Mathematics

B. Patricia Patterson

Mathematically literate students are the product of mathematically literate teachers. Mathematically literate teachers are those who understand how to engage learners in mathematical thinking to construct mathematical knowledge. Effective mathematics teachers implement and continuously monitor a purposefully orchestrated hierarchy of learning activities that intentionally facilitates students' mathematical thinking and communication about meaning to construct conceptual knowledge (Thompson, Kersaint, Richards, Hunsader, & Rubenstein, 2008).

Conceptual knowledge is the explanatory knowledge that mathematicians create, and from which they derive algorithms and mathematical proofs. While competency in calculation and ability to correctly invoke an algorithm are mathematical skills, a mathematically literate person can use their conceptual knowledge of the meaning of numbers and number theory to understand, solve, and explain, using multiple representations, the meaning of any mathematical problem or statement. Mathematicians, like every scholar working within a discipline, construct knowledge in this manner.

The goal of a constructivist classroom is to engage novice learners in the same process in which the knowledge-makers of the discipline engage. In mathematics, this process is known as mathematical thinking. The skills of mathematical thinking are well explained in early reform documents (e.g., NCTM, 2000) and in contemporary constructivist aligned texts (e.g. Thompson, et al., 2008), and in constructivist aligned mathematics curriculum.

A major limiting factor of successful implementation of the beliefs in the standards and the curriculum to which it is aligned is often the knowledge base of teachers. They lack an understanding of the nature of mathematics (White-Clark, DeCarlo, & Gilchriest, 2008).

It is a well-known maxim that we teach as we are taught. Thus effective constructivist mathematics teachers must be created by being taught through constructivist methodologies. They must become participants in a learning community engaged in mathematical thinking for the purpose of constructing and communicating mathematical knowledge (Howard, McGee, Schwartz, & Purcell, 2000; White, 2002). Without such experiences, they will teach mathematics didactically, as they were taught.

THE CHALLENGE OF CREATING CONSTRUCTIVIST MATHEMATICS TEACHERS

Teacher candidates come to their mathematics methods courses immersed in the experiences of the didactic mathematics classroom. College level mathematics courses in particular, are set up to teach the "shorthand" version of mathematics didactically. In a didactic mathematics classroom, accuracy and speed of calculation and appropriate use of algorithms are taught through direct instruction. Mathematical proofs must be couched in mathematical language, the meaning of which need not be fully or deeply understood to successfully complete a calculation and justify a proof.

In the didactic classroom mathematics "understanding" is evaluated in recall tests, the scores of which are used as an indirect measure of a student's ability to reason, problem solve, and "understand" mathematical terminology. Such learning tasks do not necessarily produce mathematically literate learners, but rather competent and "incompetent" algorithm performers who perceive themselves as being either "good" at math or "bad" at math, based on where they fall on the bell curve in their competitively structured traditional math classes.

Emphasis on mathematics as calculation has the potential to disconnect for the learner the algorithm from its developmental history - of how humans derived the language of mathematics, for what particular purposes each area of mathematics was created, and the fundamental assumptions about numbers and their relationships on which concepts about numbers were formed and principles of relationships between numbers were discovered. Such knowledge is considered essential for mathematical literacy (Sowder, Philipp, Armstrong, & Schappelle, 1998; Thompson, et al., 2008).

Thus effective constructivist mathematics teachers are not the product of their traditional mathematics classrooms. A purposeful educative intervention is necessary.

This task falls to the mathematics methods courses, taught by mathematically and mathematically pedagogically literate teachers with an expert knowledge of best constructivist practice. It is their task to change the meaning of teacher candidates' experiences with the learning and then the teaching of mathematics. They are able to do this because they have a conceptual knowledge base in mathematics; and they value and can communicate the legitimacy of the constructivist approach for learning and teaching mathematics.

A CONSTRUCTIVIST MATHEMATICS METHODS COURSE

The instructional approaches described here were developed over several semesters in a junior level undergraduate mathematics methods course required of all elementary and middle school teacher candidates at a small Mid-Atlantic college. The author/researcher developed and teaches the course and uses the outcomes as part of an ongoing line of inquiry about constructivist teacher education.

These descriptions of instructional practice and their outcomes are a snapshot in an ongoing cycle of practitioner research on the issue of how best to change the meaning of teacher candidates' experiences with mathematics learning while deepening their conceptual knowledge; and in so doing, change their perceptions and beliefs about what it means to learn and teach mathematics in the elementary and middle school classroom.

Currently, the course objective is to engage students in the customary use of mathematical thinking to generate conceptual explanations in everyday language (not "math-speak") of familiar mathematical statements (such as $1/2 \times 1/4 = 1/8$). The objective is met through the establishment and continual monitoring of three inter-woven instructional strategies that engage and monitor students in generating mathematical meaning throughout the course.

These strategies are the following:

1. Establishment of a collaborative learning community using semantic analysis learning tasks
2. Customary use of mathematical models for problem representation and meaning making
3. Recursive meta-cognitive reflection on content and process

Though used simultaneously throughout the course, each approach is described here in terms of *what the teacher does, how the students respond,* and the significant *learning outcomes* for each. Assertions in each descriptive category are drawn from ongoing constant comparative analysis of a variety of artifacts collected over the past two years. These include instructor journals, anecdotal information from classroom observation and discourse, student tests, student journals, and students' written lesson plans with embedded assessments.

STRATEGY 1 - ESTABLISHING COOPERATIVE LEARNING GOALS

What the Teacher Does

Because of teacher candidates' experiences with competitive goal structures, the mathematics methods teacher must first establish a collaborative goal structure by leveling the mathematics knowledge playing field.

Students who perceive themselves as either "good" or "bad" at math must be brought together for authentic collaboration about the meaning of mathematics. This is accomplished by changing the expectations for how learning is to take place through changing the nature of the mathematics knowledge terrain. This can be accomplished quickly when the teacher poses problems to the class, asking them to create something unfamiliar (mathematical meaning) from the familiar (mathematical algorithms).

The methods teacher poses different questions about familiar and seemingly simple mathematics problems. She does not provide ready answers to these questions, but instead asks more questions based on students' initial answers. The teacher persists in rejecting all descriptions of the problem students proffer that are couched in mathematical terms to re-direct them into collaborative sense-making that culminates in articulation of meaning of the operation using everyday language.

Through this Socratic discourse, students become engaged in semantic analysis of the meaning of common mathematical terms and operations; and as meaning is constructed, all learners are engaged in its negotiation. No one knows the "answer," and the collaborative learning context is quickly established. An example of this discourse follows:

> *In the Classroom:*
> *In one of the first lessons of the number sense unit, the instructor presents a simply solved problem, $1/2 \times 1/4 = 1/8$, and asks students what this statement means. What she is looking for is a description in everyday language of what*

has transpired between the two multiplicands, and what the solution is describing. The instructor rejects the initial math-speak student response of "one half times one fourth equals one eighth."

The instructor uses questions and acts as the "expert" in rejecting non-valid or mathematically couched descriptions of "multiplication" until students are able to describe the statement as " 1/4 of 1/2 is 1/8 th " (or vice versa). This is a valid description, but from there, the instructor must get students to provide an explanation of the outcome of the operation, again using semantic analysis to derive an explanation of why the operation of multiplication does not always produce a larger product; and to explain why the outcome is different depending upon the nature of the numbers in the operation.

Questioning is re-directed by putting a multiplication problem with whole numbers beside the fraction problem, one such as 4 X 2 = 8. The instructor then asks the class to apply their everyday description of what happens to fractions in multiplication to generate a description of what happens to whole numbers in a multiplication operation; and to compare the descriptions. Are they the same? Different? How are they the same? How are they different?

She is looking for students to notice that the product of a fraction multiplication operation is smaller than both of the fractions in the operation, but the product of the whole number operation is larger than both the whole numbers in the operation. She then poses the questions of "is this always true?" and "why"? Students work in groups to test and draw conclusions and posit answers to both questions, which are then discussed by the class, again with the instructor providing questions that re-direct thinking.

As students investigate the meaning of the operation of multiplication when different kinds of numbers are involved, the instructor continues to pose questions so that the investigation is deepened to probe the limits of the commutative property, and "why" it applies to multiplication but not division and subtraction, to investigate the nature of a fraction as a ratio, and connect their understanding of operations with decimals and percentages to the central concept of "ratio"; and to investigate the meaning of division, addition, and subtraction with all kinds of numbers.

In later units, the instructor re-visits the meaning of arithmetic operations for integers with unlike signs, always beginning with what they learned previously about these operations with whole numbers and numbers that represent ratios.

During the course of any mathematics investigation, the role of the instructor is to provide rich mathematical data from which questions can be posed. The instructor facilitates Socratic discourse, and provides information on an "as needed" basis during problem solving (White-Clarke, DeCarlo, & Gilchriest, 2008). Problem solving takes the form of semantic analysis for mathematical meaning, an unfamiliar norm in a mathematics learning environment for teacher candidates newly arrived from their didactic mathematics college courses.

Learning communities are naturally established in the classroom when no student can readily supply the answer to the questions posed by the instructor; and the instructor allows for and encourages what naturally follows – students begin to confer with one another to meet the instructor's challenge.

How the Students Respond

Students' expectations for how they should be taught and how they should learn are changed by their experiences in this learning environment. Teacher candidates come to their first mathematics methods course with an algorithmic mathematics learning experience, and as a result of their ability to follow the steps of any given algorithm to a correct solution, consider themselves to be either "good" at math or "bad" at math.

They expect the mathematics instructor to have and give all the answers and solutions, which they will mimic to the best of their ability, and be rewarded for accordingly. They arrive as passive learners, and mimic the "math-speak" of their professors when describing problems, solutions, and proofs

When asked a simple question about the meaning of a mathematical statement, neither the "good" or "bad" math students can identify or articulate in everyday language the mathematical concept or principle on which the statement is considered "true" or "false." Rather, they provide a solution to the statement, using the common algorithm and provide an explanation of the problem in "math-speak." When challenged to translate meaning of the statement into everyday language, they are brought up short.

Instantaneously there are no more "good" and "bad" math students. Everyone is "bad" at math, a phrase continually uttered from semester to semester.

Because of the unfamiliar nature of the problems posed, collaboration to negotiate meaning quickly becomes the norm. The terrain of mathematical learning has changed. It is unfamiliar to all.

Often it is students who have had the least success in traditional math classes who emerge as leaders in discussions when the learning norm is shifted from memorizing algorithms to understanding mathematical principles. In fact, they state that this is what they have been looking for in their traditional mathematics classes.

On the other hand, the students who have, until this course, considered themselves "good" at math, react differently. Initially they deny the legitimacy of the questions, and cling to algorithmic solutions couched in mathematical terminology. Their comments include such statements as "this isn't math," or "why can't we just work it the way we know how?"

However, when both groups are successful for the first time in understanding a mathematical principle as members of a collaborative group, the meaning of their experiences with mathematics learning begins to change, as do their comments. Both groups converge on such statements as "so what have we been learning all along?" or "why don't they teach us THIS in math class?"

Learning Outcomes

Students learn from these semantic analysis exercises that the only acceptable way to demonstrate their mathematical knowledge is to "translate" the meaning of any mathematical statement into everyday language. Use of math terms such as "times," "least common denominator," "and equivalent fraction" must be subjected to semantic analysis in which definitions are derived in everyday language; and relationships between numbers in mathematical operations are explained based on the characteristics and properties of the numbers in the operation and of the operation itself.

This strategy is used in every unit of study in the course, and students quickly adjust to this expectation and display a heightened sense of engagement in the collaborative group. Every "new" problem set brings unfamiliar territory; and collaborative sense-making becomes a necessity.

From the first lesson on the meaning of number, to the final lesson on Geometric patterns in art, teacher candidates in the course come to routinely depend on one another to negotiate mathematical meaning of familiar mathematical statements using semantic analysis, until they are able to routinely look for and derive meaning from less familiar and progressively more complex mathematical statements (see Table 2.1 for the problem set list and target concepts and principles used in the whole group setting).

Students quickly realize they are in this together, and must depend upon one another for the "answer" rather than the instructor, who is only there to let them know how they are doing, and if they are on the right track.

"Can't you just tell us the answer" is a common phrase during the initial activities, but such a question becomes less common as they continue to work through these problems, until the question is extinguished by the end of the semester. In fact, when tested by the instructor toward the middle of the semester, when she says "ok, do you want me to tell you?" They look up only briefly to say "NO, we'll get it". Such responses lead to the conclusion that students have come to value the collaborative goal structure for learning.

Table 2.1. Engaging Problems in Semantic Analysis of Critical Mathematical Concepts and Principles

Target Mathematical Concept	Problem Posed by Instructor	Outcome/Assessed Product
Number	Instructor presents a list of many different kinds of numbers to the class, and asks the students to describe each, pushes them to connect each to a use in the "real world"; use everyday language to describe, and describe relationships between each, as they create categories of numbers, as well as further examples of each kind of number.	Hierarchical concept map that demonstrates valid connections between and among all types of numbers, supported by explanatory text that defines the meaning and use of each number type in everyday language, and the whole group's collective voice.
Place Value	Alternate base addition and subtraction mathematical statements are presented to the group. Meaning of the numbers, their values, and patterns of relationships between value and grouping rule are explored during whole and small group discussions.	Students collaborate on a definition of place value that reflects the role of grouping rules for the value of a place; and can use this explanation appropriately and customarily when justifying solutions to other problems.
Ratio	Instructor presents a "list" of numbers represented as fractions, decimals, ratios, and percents and asks students to describe the numbers and their meaning.	Group produces a hierarchical concept map for fractions that defines them as a ratio, contains other critical characteristics of fractions as well as connections to decimals, proportions, and percentages.
Whole Number Division and Multiplication	Instructor asks students to explain the meaning of the following everyday statements: "multiplication is a shortcut to addition"; "division undoes multiplication"; "division is like subtraction"; and to describe a whole number division problem partitively and distributively, posing the question as to why two approaches to a problem can yield the same "answer".	Students are expected to generate everyday language descriptions of common arithmetic statements and use these in their personal mathematics journals to customarily describe problems.

Arithmetic Operations with Fractions	Instructor asks students to compare the outcomes of a set of whole number multiplication and division problems to the outcomes of a set of fraction multiplication and division problems, and explain why the outcomes are different.	Students are expected to use what they learned about the meaning of whole number arithmetic operations to understand and communicate the meaning of arithmetic operations with fractions. And to explain WHY and HOW the operations and their outcomes differ.
The Zero Principle	Students are asked to explain the commonly used rules that can predict the sign of an arithmetic operation with integers of like and unlike signs, rather than just state the rules.	Students are expected to use graphical models beyond that of a number line (i.e., red and black pieces) to demonstrate the validity of the zero principle as an explanation of the sign of an integer that is the result of any arithmetic operation.
Constant	Students are asked to work backwards through a variety of algebraic formulae that have constants (including the formula for finding the circumference and then the area of a circle).	Students are expected to generate explanations of the role of a constant in any quantitative relationship.
Dimension	Students use the formula or an area for a circle to generate an explanation/justification for the formulae that represents the area of volume.	Students are able to identify patterns of relatedness based on formulae, between lines, planes, and 3-dimensional shapes.
Polygon	Students are given a variety of different triangles and asked to sort and classify them according to their geometric properties.	Students create a "tree" or concept map that demonstrates the variety of categories of triangles and the degree of their relatedness, based on their geometric properties, providing examples of each.

Using the familiar to create new learning territory by looking for meaning in mathematical statements rather than describing the algorithmic solutions is a successful strategy to create instant collaboration. Competitive goal structures do not work when every learner is on unfamiliar learning terrain, and when they look to the teacher for the "answer," she simply poses another question or provides another "fact" that changes the finality of the answer and throws the problem back to them.

A further outcome is that students form collaborative work groups outside of class. The second customary teaching strategy assures that this will happen when unfamiliar mathematical models are introduced as visual "props" for generating meaning.

STRATEGY 2 - CUSTOMARY USE OF MATHEMATICAL MODELS

What the Teacher Does

To break students' perceptions of the algorithm as the whole of mathematical knowledge, the instructor utilizes a variety of concrete, semi-abstract, and abstract models for representation of mathematical relationships. She requires that students represent all problems in multiple formats, and overtly teaches students to use these models as tools, to enhance their semantic analysis of mathematical meaning.

> *In the Classroom:*
> *In the Number Sense unit, place value is a major target concept. Cuisenaire rods are used to help students un-couple the meaning of place value from the base 10 numeration system, so that valid meaning of this critical foundational concept can be derived.*
>
> *The instructor begins this lesson with the presentation of two simple addition problems, such as 3+2 = 5 and 15 + 12 = 27. She then asks students to represent both the problem and the solution using the Cuisenaire rods. After several more "practice" problems, and making sure students can articulate the relationship between the rods and their value, and can demonstrate the correct procedure for representing addition problems and their solutions with them, she says elicits responses about the use of the 10 rod, when it is used and what the numbers in the 10's place represent (2 10's, 1 10, etc.).*
>
> *She says... "So now we know how to use the Cuisenaire Rods to show the meaning of place value... ok... let's try to represent this problem"... she writes an alternate base problem on the board, such as 12 3 +14 6 = _____ 7, and asks students to use the rods to represent all three numbers in the problem. She asks them to describe this problem; and corrects them until they are able to say 1-2 base 3 is being added to 1-4 base 6, and the solution should be represented in base 7."*

From this investigation, the instructor guides students into pursuing subtraction, multiplication and division with alternate base numbers, to deepen an understanding of the role of place value in arithmetic operations and their outcomes. The instructor continually re-visits, through questioning, and recording progressively different definitions for evaluation of the concept of place value until students can generalize about the relationship between grouping rules and the value of a place in any given number. All mathematical models used in the course are listed in Table 2.2.

How the Students Respond

When presented with an alternative base problem such as the one above, students at first are unable to describe the problem correctly. They say "twelve base 3" plus 14 base 6." Once they have been corrected on this description and are able to describe the numbers in the problem, they are asked to represent this new problem and its solution with the rods. Because the instructor did not provide the solution to the problem, they immediately abandon the Cuisenaire rods and try to solve the problem algorithmically, trying to recall the "factoring" trick they were taught in their mathematics classes (though they are not sure why this works, when asked, some of them can still remember how to do it).

Since the instructor re-focuses the students on the actual learning task, which is to represent the problem with the Cuisenaire rods, students are forced to confer within their groups. Through discussion, trial and error, and working backwards to negotiate the meaning of the problem, they succeed in utilizing the correct rods to represent the place values of all three numbers.

They arrive at the representation, in which the 3 rod and 6 rod is used to represent the number in the "10's" place of the two addends and the 7 rod is used as the "10's" place in representing the sum. This takes a considerable amount of time and continual instructor feedback and questioning.

Once students have succeeded in representing and describing the initial problem, they always request more, and are given a variety of problems of both addition, as well as subtraction. Throughout their representation struggles, they must re-visit the meaning of place value to create valid representations of the alternate base mathematical statements.

They always ask "what about multiplication and division?" and as they explore these operations with alternate bases, the meaning of the operations of multiplication and division become clearer: Multiplication and division deal essentially with a single number – how it is added to itself multiple times or, when divided, how it is split into groups (distributively or partitively).

Learning Outcomes

Engagement in the representation of alternative base problems with Cuisenaire rods results in an expanded personal meaning of the concept of place value.

As a result of their experiences, students are able to generate deep explanations of the relationship between place and a number's value and use these explanations as referents when they are asked to order numbers in different bases from least to greatest and justify their ordering; and when they are asked to create addition tables in different bases, and analyze the outcomes for patterns based on grouping rules (and later to derive an algebraic formula that generalizes the relationship between grouping rules and number value). When they are asked to examine the interaction of numbers represented in alternate bases in other arithmetic operations they can explain what happens to the numbers and why.

The use of models continues as other targeted concepts and principles are considered; and reactions remain the same. Students become adept at customary use of alternative concrete or semi-abstract models for visualizing relationships of numbers to one another in mathematical problems and statements. Data from students' personal journals and tests indicate that they become adept at using such representations to reason through to meaning, provide visual proof, or answer a "why" question about the relationships residing within the numbers of a mathematical problem or statement.

Table 2.2 describes the models used with each of the course's target concepts and the accompanying learner outcomes that were assessed in a variety of student products, including personal mathematics journals, formal tests, and anecdotal running records.

STRATEGY 3 - RECURSIVE META-COGNITIVE REFLECTION ON CONTENT AND PROCESS

What the Teacher Does

The teacher emphasizes the need for students to focus on their own mental processes during mathematics investigations. The instructor provides a framework of a thinking process during mathematical inquiry, and routinely engages students in focusing on the level of thinking in which they are engaging both at the conclusion of, and during a mathematics investigation activity. Broadly, the instructor wants students to differentiate between de-

Table 2.2 Mathematical Models

Target Concept or Principle	Mathematical Model	Learner Outcome
Number	Cuisenaire Rods	Use rods to represent operations of addition and subtraction of whole numbers as a basis for generating explanations of the relationship of numbers to one another in the number set.
Place Value	Locking cubes Cuisenaire Rods Napier's Bones	Describe the relationship between place, grouping rule, and value of a multi-digit number.
Whole Number Division and Multiplication	Cuisenaire Rods Napier's Bones Multiplication Charts	Analyze a variety of semi-abstract and alternative computational models for patterns of relatedness between operation and outcome, unrelated to the traditional algorithm.
Ratio, Equivalency	Cuisenaire Rods and Fraction Circles	Analyze a visual representation of parts of whole to generate an explanation of fractions as ratios of parts to wholes, and thus an explanation of equivalency based on an understanding of ratio, not "factors" and "lcd"s per se.
Arithmetic Operations with Fractions	Cuisenaire Rods	Analyze operations with fractions to "discover" that arithmetic operations only occur in the numerators of fractions, and justify the need for a common denominator that is not related to "LCD" or "GCF."

The Zero Principle	Red and Black Pieces	Analyze the outcomes of addition, subtraction, and multiplication of integers with opposite and the same signs to derive the meaning of the zero principle.
Combining Algebraic Expressions	Algebra Tiles	Use algebra tiles to demonstrate knowledge of algebraic expressions and the zero principle to analyze and create representations of algebraic expression before and after they are combined.
Constant	A variety of different sized circles	Derive Pi through analysis of the direct measure of the diameter and radius of circles of different sizes.
The relationship between area and volume	Student-constructed nets Solid and "empty" shape sets	Apply geometric reasoning to the design of a two-dimensional net that, when cut out and assembled makes a three dimensional shape. Generate an explanation of the relationship between the formulae for area and for volume of a variety of shapes.
Polygon	A variety of different types of triangles	Through direct measure of angles and sides, generate categories of triangles, and then determine the name of each type, using text and mathematical dictionaries.

scriptive, transformational, explanatory, and evaluative knowledge, and to understand how the categories are interdependent in the knowledge-making process.

The principles of Dewey's "authentic" inquiry as practically interpreted by Gowin (1981) and others were used to create a representation of the knowledge-making process (Description, Transformation, Explanation, Evaluation) as well as a benchmarked rubric used to assess written student reflections (See Text Box 2.1 and Appendix). When students are asked to write mathematics lessons late in this course, and routinely in their senior mathematics courses, they are expected to use these sections as a guide for planning learner activities that are tightly scripted and contain embedded assessments at each level of thinking.

> Text Box 2.1
> The Knowledge-Making Process in Mathematics
> *Describe* mathematical statements in everyday language. (WHAT?)
> Analyze (*transform*) familiar mathematical statements, equations, and algorithms for meaning. (HOW?)
> Use everyday language to *explain* mathematical statements in terms of concepts and principles rather than in terms of the steps of the algorithm. (WHY?)
> Use criteria from the discipline to *evaluate* your own knowledge and to generate questions that guide further mathematical inquiry. (WHAT IF?)

Students are required to keep a personal mathematics journal as a major course product. In the journal they must demonstrate through rich descriptions of their problem solving and reasoning how they continue their personal lines of mathematical inquiry beyond the collaborative classroom setting and how they incorporate mathematically valid conceptual (explanatory) knowledge into mathematical proofs.

Teacher candidates in the course have the opportunity to observe the instructor's strategies, and purposeful discussion of these strategies at the conclusion of each class engages students in thinking about their thinking during the activities of the lesson. The knowledge-making process is placed on the board, and students are asked to dissect the lesson they just engaged in by category of thinking they were doing, (and, what the teacher did to get them to do that kind of thinking).

They are also asked to consider the nature of the "data" the instructor provided... was it a worksheet? The idea of generating sense-making around a single "deep" problem or problem set is continually re-visited.

How Students Respond

Students have had scant, if any experience recording their thinking about the meaning of mathematics, so they find this expectation a difficult one to meet, even with explicit modeling and consistent re-visiting of the process using the graphical representation. Early personal learning journal entries are predominantly given over to a description of the steps of solving a particular problem; or descriptions of how models are used to represent problems with few, if any records that demonstrate thinking about meaning (see Excerpts in Table 2.3).

Later journal entries, however, become more authentically reflective, and begin to demonstrate the emergence of mathematical thinking for conceptual knowledge construction. In later entries, students record more substantive questions that are directly related to the problem they are working on. They more frequently extend their thinking about a problem to the "why" or explanation, and can use conceptual mathematical principles or conceptual definitions as justification for an outcome.

The difference between answers on the first quiz and the final examination is also noticeable, as excerpts from these artifacts demonstrate (see Table 2.3). Students are able to use valid conceptual principles to justify the outcome of a problem, and use semantic analysis to understand the meaning of a problem and "translate" from mathematical representation to everyday language.

A shift in the ability to apply their newly honed mathematical thinking skills to lesson plans is the ultimate test of their ability to reflect, given that this is a methods course. Examples of early and late lesson plans are also provided in Table 2.3. Students are able to shift from teaching procedures to using models and good questions to assist children in constructing mathematical knowledge through mathematical thinking.

Learning Outcomes

Because journals are continually monitored with continual written and oral feedback from the teacher, entries begin to become more focused on the thinking about meaning, rather than describing the steps of the algorithm. Examples of early and late entries may be seen in Table 2.3.

Teacher candidates are expected to write lesson plans with embedded assessments and to deliver several of them in the practicum that accompanies this methods course. In comparing first to last lesson plans as well as their evaluations from observers, growth toward the constructivist teaching paradigm is demonstrated. Teacher candidates become more adept at choosing exemplar problems, engaging learners in seeking answers to probing questions, facilitating collaboration for meaning-making, and using models to both assess and facilitate their students' making of mathematical meaning.

Table 2.3. Excerpts that Demonstrate Growth in Mathematical Thinking

Student Artifact	Early Responses/Excerpts	Late Responses/Excerpts
Personal Mathematics Journal	"greatest common factor is important in reducing fractions" (mathspeak, no "why") "whole number addition involves two addends and a sum (mathspeak only) "multiplication is addition with factors" (mathspeak) "to add fractions with the C-rods, you have to line up the denominators and make them equal" (procedural talk)	"this problem is a division problem with fractions, so it is asking how many 2/3's are in 5/8" (use of everyday language to describe the meaning of a problem) "I know that the area of a rectangle is found by multiplying the length by the width, - one dimension by the other... can I think about the area of a circle in the same way? What is the circle's length? Its circumference? Then what is its width? Hmmm...." (mathematical reasoning)
Test Question: "Represent this statement mathematically and tell what mathematical principle was employed to find the solution: "the number of 3/7 in 2/3"...	Quiz One response: Represented as a multiplication rather than a division problem. Principle cited as "common denominator" and "commutative property."	Final Exam (different problem but same type) Represented as a division of fractions problem, with the principle cited and explained as "equivalencies of ratios," explained why the "answer" was larger than the two fractions involved in the operation.
Lesson Plan Assignment: "Create a lesson plan for Grades 1-2 that incorporates the use of Cuisenaire rods for understanding the operation of addition of whole positive numbers."	Focus Question: How may Cuisenaire Rods can be used to represent Addition? (Procedural, around use of the model)	Focus Question: What happens to whole positive numbers when they are added? (Cuisenaire Rods used to help students analyze relationships between the numbers in the problems and use to generalize an answer to the focus question).

CONCLUSION

If it is true that we teach as we were taught, then to teach as constructivists, teacher candidates must have the opportunity to learn as constructivists. Their mathematics learning must be slowed down and re-directed toward conceptual understanding.

They must learn the authentic mathematical concepts and principles behind the algorithms they learned how to use in their math classes. They must be taught to engage in the processes of reasoning and problem solving, not just taught "about" them, or "how" to teach them. They must be taught to connect previous mathematical knowledge to "new" mathematical knowledge. Collaboration must be engaged in to negotiate the meaning of mathematical language and to communicate that meaning in the everyday language they will need in order to share meaning with their students.

The learning activities described in this chapter are used in a junior level mathematics methods course to accomplish all of these learning goals. Collaborative goal structures, customary use of mathematical models, and focused reflection on meta-cognition during problem solving are strategies used in the course to change the meaning of the experience of what it means to learn mathematics, and transform teacher candidates into mathematically literate teachers.

As a result of their first-hand experiences with learning mathematics through the process of mathematical thinking, teacher candidates are afforded the opportunity to become empowered, not just as "native" speakers of mathematical language (able to use math terms meaningfully), but also as translators of the meaning of mathematical language and learning for their students, using the learning experiences in this course as a constructivist teaching model.

As stated in the introduction, these strategies and their outcomes represent a snapshot in an ongoing effort to change the meaning of teacher candidates' experiences with the learning and teaching of mathematics. Over the course of several semesters, the strategies and outcomes described here have evolved, and will continue to do so as the instructor engages in further analysis and reflection about the outcomes.

These instructional approaches, however, have shown promise in shifting perceptions, beliefs, and practices of prospective elementary and middle school mathematics teachers toward the constructivist teaching paradigm; and other methods instructors are invited to implement, test, and refine them.

REFERENCES

Gowin, D.B. (1981). *Educating*. Ithaca, NY: Cornell University Press.

Howard, B., McGee, S., Schwartz, N., & Purcell, S. (2000). The experience of constructivism: Transforming teacher epistemology. *Journal of Research on Computing in Education, 32*(4), 455 – 465.

National Council of Teachers of Mathematics (NCTM) (2000). *Principles and standards for school mathematics*. Reston, VA: NCTM.

Sowder, J. T., Philipp, R.A., Armstrong, B.E., & Schappelle, B.P. (1998). *Middle-grade teachers' mathematical knowledge and its relationship to instruction. A Research Monograph*. New York: State University of New York Press.

Thompson, D.R., Kersaint, G., Richards, J.C., Hunsader, P.D., & Rubenstein, R.N. (2008). *Mathematical literacy: Helping students make meaning in the middle grades*. Portsmouth, NH: Heinemann.

White, Bonita C. (2002). Constructing constructivist teaching: Reflection as research. *Reflective Practice, 3* (2), 307-326.

White-Clarke, R., DeCarlo, M., & Gilchrist, Sister N. (2008). Guide on the side: An instructional approach to meet mathematics standards. *The High School Journal, April/May*, 40-44.

APPENDIX

Reflection Rubric for Mathematical Thinking in the Personal Mathematical Journal

Scoring Scale

1 = no evidence for indicator, unacceptable;

2 = some evidence for indicator, passing but needs improvement;

3 = acceptable evidence for indicator, meets minimum course requirements but not professionally ready;

4 = regular evidence for indicator, professionally ready, novice teacher candidate;

5 = exceptional evidence for indicator, professionally ready meritorious teacher candidate

Descriptive Knowledge
Definition of the Descriptive Knowledge Construct

Descriptive knowledge is factual knowledge generated and recorded by the learner as a result of experience with a primary data source (experiential, iconic, or abstract). Rich descriptive knowledge should be recorded to create records – the beginning point for knowledge construction.

Descriptive Knowledge Benchmark for the Mathematics Journal

Reflective journals in ED 303 should contain rich and diverse descriptive knowledge entries that describe exemplar problems in mathematical and non-mathematical language. In this course, journal entries are the *authentic trail of evidence* that demonstrates the foundational step in personal mathematical knowledge re-construction and learning to think mathematically.

Indicators

The journal author should:

Write mathematically valid descriptions of exemplar problems in non-mathematical terms 1 2 3 4 5
Represent problems abstractly as well as concretely and semi-abstractly 1 2 3 4 5
Provide labels for all representations 1 2 3 4 5
Record thinking in depth at every step 1 2 3 4 5

TRANSFORMATIONAL KNOWLEDGE

Definition of the Transformational Knowledge Construct

Transformational knowledge is knowledge of how to categorize, sort, organize, and find patterns of likes and differences among a set of facts. Transformational knowledge serves as the bridge between describing a single event or object, and the formation of concepts. Concepts are abstract representations with critical, recognizable attributes that serve as a mode of categorizing, and thus making sense of, seemingly disparate bits of factual knowledge. Humans communicate by means of concepts, which are the building blocks of principles and theories. Thus concepts must have precise meaning grounded in objective and deep analysis of rich sets of accurately recorded facts.

Transformational Knowledge Benchmark for the Mathematics Journal

Reflective journals in ED 303 should contain written and graphic evidence of the ability to use the process skills employed by mathematicians (NCTM standards) to analyze exemplar mathematical representations for their meaning. Appropriate in-depth analytical strategies should creditably lead to personal knowledge construction of explanatory concepts and principles that connect one form of mathematics to another, and upon which algorithms and rules of operation rest.

Indicators

The journal author should:

Use words, and a range of appropriate mathematical models and representations to document thinking during analysis of problems for meaning
1 2 3 4 5
Document an authentic problem solving orientation (understands problem, chooses appropriate strategy, employs the strategy, describes and explains the outcome, evaluates the strategy) 1 2 3 4 5
Document reasoning by comparing outcomes from problem to problem
1 2 3 4 5
Document reasoning throughout all steps in analysis of a problem for meaning 1 2 3 4 5
Apply previous knowledge to analysis of a given problem 1 2 3 4 5
Generate testable interpretative statements (mathematical conjectures) that authentically emerge from analysis of the meaning of the problem
1 2 3 4 5

EXPLANATORY KNOWLEDGE

Definition of the Explanatory Knowledge Construct

Explanatory knowledge is a set of generalized statements that emerge from the knowledge construction process through analysis of exemplar data. Explanatory statements offer reasons for observed patterns, relationships or regularities. Explanatory statements should reflect valid personal understanding of the critical concepts, principles, and theories of a discipline.

Explanatory Knowledge Benchmark for the Mathematics Journal

Reflective journals in ED 303 should demonstrate the author's competency at connecting in-depth analysis of problems to the explanations they generate about the origin of mathematical rules, and the underlying mathematical principles that determine correct mathematical solutions, specific patterns of relationships, and algorithms.

Indicators

The journal author should:

Generate mathematical conjectures that leads successive analyses toward an explanatory goal 1 2 3 4 5
Derive culminating explanatory declarative knowledge statements that justify rules, outcomes, and relationships in problem sets 1 2 3 4 5
Set up alternative problems that test mathematical conjectures arising from analysis of the meaning of a problem 1 2 3 4 5

EXTENDING KNOWLEDGE AND EVALUATIVE KNOWLEDGE

Definition of the Extending and Evaluative Knowledge Construct

Extending Knowledge is the ability to choose appropriate alternate data and contexts that test generalizable limits of explanatory statements. Evaluative knowledge is the ability to objectively examine records of knowledge construction processes and the quality and limits of the explanatory knowledge it produced.

Extending and Evaluating Benchmark for the Mathematics Journal

Reflective journals in ED 303 should demonstrate the author's level of competency at re-visiting previous analyses and conjectures to identify a starting point for the analytical steps or the next investigative question. This should result in a connected whole within the journal that documents the author's emerging ability to build and connect mathematical knowledge, to evaluate the quality of conjectures, problem solving, reasoning and communication using acquired criteria from the discipline.

Indicators

The journal author should:

> Test the limits of newly formed explanatory principles derived from one problem set with other problem sets or contexts 1 2 3 4 5
> Classify previous journal entries as descriptive, transformative or explanatory 1 2 3 4 5
> Write periodic summaries of previous knowledge 1 2 3 4 5
> Write evaluations of their descriptive, transformational and explanatory knowledge in previous entries 1 2 3 4 5

Turning Point: Lost and Found

Jamie Whitman-Smithe, Teacher Educator

I had a student who barely made it through her freshman year in college. She passed my course but had difficulty completing assignments and getting them turned in on time. She was absent from class often, and when she did attend, she participated rarely. During one class research project, however, she shared that her father had died in an accident during the summer. She was hurting. That helped me understand why she was not making the transition to "college student" very well. I was disappointed but not surprised when she did not return to school the following year.

One year later, however, this student appeared in another of my classes looking like a completely different person. There was determination in the eyes that met mine. She said that during her year out of college she had frequently thought about the concepts and lessons from my class. She told me she now understood the purpose of the assignments that involved group work, and why the course packets explained expectations giving a myriad of examples. She had thought back to her observations in a day care center and how I encouraged her to reflect on her experiences. "Now I get it!" she cried.

I'm not sure *she* truly understands what it is she "gets" quite yet, but *I* know it's constructivist teaching. She sees how the organization I provide allows students to explore a concept and come up with their own conclusions. She has noticed that some of the course guidelines, which at first seem restrictive, in reality support students in producing their best work. She says she wants to be a teacher like me. I'm honored, of course, but my wish for her is that she create her own unique, teaching life.

This student is now on a steady path to becoming a change agent in her own classroom. She cares about how students learn and how she can help them in a constructivist manner. And I am more committed to investing my time and expertise and patience in all my students, even the ones that I may end up losing. After all, you never know who might be "found" again.

Chapter Three

Writing Workshop for Teacher Candidates

Jill E. Cole

Over the years, writing workshop has become a living, breathing thing, taking different shapes for different teachers. The writing that goes on in the classroom during writing workshop can vary from self-selected writing to prompt writing, from memoirs to comic books, and from fiction to five-paragraph essays. So, what *is* writing workshop and how should it be used effectively in the classroom? These questions impelled this inquiry into the efficacy of using writing workshop to prepare future teachers to be effective teachers of writing.

It was time to revisit the roots of writing workshop. Returning to the definitions established by such foundational writing educators as Nancie Atwell, Lucy Calkins, and Donald Graves seemed a good place to begin. Why was writing workshop developed? How was it implemented? What worked and why? And then, perhaps, the question could be asked about the efficacy of using writing workshop with teacher candidates to demonstrate the writing process as well as how to teach writing effectively.

THE ROOTS OF WRITING WORKSHOP

Nancie Atwell tells the story of how she began to use writing workshop in the classroom in her classic text *In the Middle* (1987). She started by looking at her own writing and found that she did the following:

- Made choices about what to write
- Sought out resources (including people) for help and advice

- Wrote for a real audience
- Created drafts (sometimes several) before writing a final copy
- Desired to share her writing with others

In the classroom, she allowed students to be her teachers, listening to their stories and observing their writing. As she changed from a traditional writing teacher to one who led writing workshops, she states that for her and her students, writing became "less a program than a way of life" (1987, p. 17). She described writing workshop as messy and constantly changing but driven by shared beliefs. Seven principles about what writers need provided the bedrock for Atwell's teaching of writing (1987, pp. 17-18):

1. Regularly scheduled time to write is needed to form ideas, take risks with drafts, and write to a real audience.
2. Self-selected topics are important for helping students find their voice and engage in their work.
3. Response from the teacher and peers support students in the writing process.
4. Conventions are learned through the experience of meaningful writing while using a variety of resources to meet the needs of the specific piece.
5. Teachers who write can share their own personal process with students, providing a role model for the joys and challenges of writing.
6. Students and teachers need to read widely and deeply to inform their writing and to learn about other writers and writing possibilities.
7. Through reading and writing and researching, teachers must constantly learn new things about writing to meet students' needs.

Atwell never promises that writing workshop will make teaching easier. There is a lot for the teacher to sort out: ascertaining and meeting students' needs, keeping track of writers' progress, pacing minilessons, finding appropriate publishing outlets, and the list can go on and on. But teaching *will* be more meaningful, motivational, and effective. Students (and teachers) *will* become creators of real ideas and writers of original works.

Graves (1983) reminds us that writing is a craft. It requires modeling by a knowledgeable other, practicing through drafts, refining the final product, and displaying the completed piece.

Teaching writing is a craft as well. Teachers organize the classroom to support writing by supplying the space and materials. They write themselves to show students their personal writing process. They conference with students to tease out ideas, promote sustained writing, listen to revision ideas, and to teach editing on the spot. And they feel the urge to share their own writing just as they encourage students to share and publish writing outside the classroom.

Along with Atwell and Graves, Calkins (1986) also taught and observed and learned about writing workshop in real classrooms. She calls writing, and the teaching of writing, an "art," which evokes activity which is creative, innovative, emotional, personal and authentic.

Calkins suggests that perhaps we don't need more strategies and worksheets and prompts, but instead we should think of writing stripped down to its basic, inherent purposes. Why do people write? To share a story. To share themselves. To connect with the world around them. To create. "Writing is lifework, not deskwork" says Calkins (1986, p. 7). How can we as teachers enable our students to write like this? The use of a consistent writing workshop can produce this kind of writing.

Other teacher/authors who influenced the philosophy of writing workshop are Andrea Butler and Jan Turbill, Georgia Heard, and Frank Smith. Butler and Turbill (1987) emphasize that reading and writing are intertwined and affect each other. We should teach our students to read with the mindset of a writer, and to write using what they have learned through reading.

Frank Smith (1983) may have been one of the first to recognize that children learn to read and write by reading and writing. Perhaps this is true of teacher candidates as well. Many of them express fear of writing or a certainty that they can't write well. They report not doing much writing throughout their schooling, and the writing they did was prescriptive and formal. Smith would encourage them to develop their own personal writing habit as they learn to encourage their future students to do the same.

Finally, it is often poetry that first convinces students that they have something to say and that they *can* write after all. Georgia Heard (1989) expresses joy in her writing and for the teaching of writing. She lets teachers know that they can inspire students to write by focusing on personal experience, strong feelings, and the heart. Writing workshop is a framework which can allow for this kind of satisfying, important writing.

WRITING WORKSHOP BROUGHT UP-TO-DATE

The literature of the 1980s and 1990s described writing workshop richly and in detail. Accordingly, the Literacy Dictionary (Harris & Hodges, 1995) defines writing workshop as "a block of school time devoted to student planning, drafting, and editing compositions for publication, often involving peer collaboration" (p. 284).

But what does current literature say? While professional development materials for teachers often stray from the original intent of the writing workshop format (they may use the term however), strong support was found for the kind of writing workshop originally espoused by Atwell, Graves, Calkins, and colleagues.

Tompkins (2006) and Anderson (2000) concur that the components of writing workshop include minilessons taught by the teacher, self-selected independent writing, student-teacher conferences, sharing with peers, and publishing. Minilessons often focus on getting ideas for writing, grammar issues, revising and editing, and avenues for publishing. Independent writing offers students the experience of going through the writing process: prewriting, drafting, revising, editing, and sharing writing with appropriate audiences. Tompkins also encourages teachers to read aloud to model good writing.

The workshop framework has its challenges. Overmeyer's book *When Writing Workshop Isn't Working* (2005) addresses these concerns. He provides suggestions for teachers on thorny issues such as finding time for writing workshop, managing conferences, planning for instruction, and assessing student writing. However, he iterates that the best way to teach writing is to have students write – not fill in blanks on a worksheet – but really write. Students must grapple with writing on their own to learn and improve.

Overmeyer emphasizes that writing workshop inspires in students a passion for sharing stories, talking about writing, and examining other authors' work. There is no program that can tap into the specific needs and interests of student writers like writing workshop. Weber (2002) also reminds us of the importance of opening up the passion of writing to *all* our students, including second-language learners and struggling students.

Recent research shows that process-oriented writing instruction, like writing workshop, improves student achievement in writing (Whitney, Blau, Bright, Cabe, Dewar, Levin, Macias, & Rogers, 2010). The authors state that process writing is a philosophical stance as well as a set of activities. In research that compared two teachers using the same writing lessons in their classrooms, the teacher with the process-oriented philosophy of writing demonstrated higher achievement in her students' writing. Helping teachers develop a philosophy of how students learn to write is essential.

Cappello (2010) asserts that the definitive goal of education is producing independent learners. We say this often but don't often provide the means to help students achieve it. Writing workshop is designed to provide the guidance, practice, skills, and structure to promote independent writing.

The National Commission of Writing in America's Schools and Colleges published a report on *The Neglected "R": The Need for a Writing Revolution* in 2003. The report noted that the NAEP (National Assessment of Educational Progress) shows that students basically know language and can write when necessary; however, they lack higher levels of writing skills which include critical writing and sophistication of language. In response to this, the Commission set four challenges that need to be addressed: providing time for writing, assessing student writing effectively, integrating technology into writing, and supporting the teaching of writing in the classroom.

The Commission calls writing an art. Time is needed to practice and hone an art. Assessment must be appropriate (and probably different than it is now). Technology should expand the experiences students have in writing. And teachers certainly need support to be writers themselves so they can authentically teach writing to their students. Writing workshop can provide both the philosophy and framework to support teaching writing as an art.

An important problem that was uncovered by the Commission was that most preservice and inservice teachers have not had the opportunity to see themselves as writers or experience the satisfaction of writing for self-expression or as access to learning. They need the passion before they can inspire passion in their students.

The Commission calls for colleges and universities to remedy this situation – they must teach more writing! In this chapter I propose just that. We must immerse teacher candidates in writing for themselves before we can train them to teach their future students to write. The bottom line is that teachers must be change agents for writing in the classroom.

These are the pieces to the puzzle of writing workshop. The question then is, how do we get them to "fit" into the structure and discourse of the classroom?

WRITING WORKSHOP IN THE COLLEGE CLASSROOM

Writing workshop helps teacher candidates develop a passion for writing and enables them to teach writing workshop in their own future classrooms. It also fits comfortably into the typical college/university schedule. Whether the class meets once, twice, or three times a week, all the components of writing workshop can be accommodated and practiced each class period. These components include a minilesson, independent writing, conferencing, and publication.

Minilessons

The minilesson is taught by the instructor of the course at the beginning of each class and usually lasts 10-30 minutes. "Mini" refers to the fact that the lesson is narrowly focused on one writing issue, not necessarily short in duration. Minilessons present foundational background information and address a myriad of topics.

At the beginning of the semester, the minilesson provides a definition of writing workshop, how each class period will be organized, or hints about keeping a writer's notebook (class notes, writing ideas, rough drafts) that becomes a resource for future teaching. As the semester gets underway, strategies for collecting good writing ideas are paramount. This can be the hardest part of writing. Students *and* candidates, regardless of grade level, need guidance in learning how to look around themselves to see all the possibilities. They need help noticing the small details that are crucial to good description or delving into their lives to dig out a noteworthy memoir.

An Idea Book allows candidates to record their discoveries and thoughts. Ideas may take the form of interesting words, topics, sketches, diary entries, descriptions, lists, quotes, or snatches of conversations. The ideas may also be tactile - objects such as a button, post card, flower petal, or train ticket are kept in an Idea "Box."

Mentor texts are used in minilessons to highlight a particular literary technique. For example, by reading aloud an excerpt from Maya Angelou's book, *Why the Caged Bird Sings,* the instructor demonstrates how to turn a childhood memory into a story. Poetry and picture books are used to show effective leads and conclusions, vivid vocabulary, character development, or rising action. The advantage of short texts such as these is that they allow candidates to see a whole piece of literature in one class session (e.g., lead, rising action, resolution, theme). Newspaper or magazine articles, pamphlets, brochures, how-to books, or travel books are used to demonstrate nonfiction.

While all kinds of literature can be used as mentor texts, using children's literature serves a dual purpose. It demonstrates the specific writing element that the instructor wants to show the teacher candidates, and is an example of literature appropriate for candidates to use with children. For the duration of the course, candidates keep a Mentor Text List of children's books which includes specific titles along with their connections to writing.

Some minilessons lay out the structure and expectations for candidate-instructor conferences. They ensure that candidates are prepared for the conference with sufficient rough draft work and a list of specific questions.

Minilessons also address peer conferences. It is important that these conferences are structured and solution-directed, so they don't turn into a conversation about last night's football game or simply sink into silence. Preparation can be as simple as one or more questions that are important to the writer and the responders. (Refer to Appendix A for a sample Peer Conferencing Form.) Then the candidates can work on a plan of action together.

Toward the end of the semester when candidates begin to publish their writing, minilessons focus on revising and editing. Time is allowed especially for revision since candidates tend to see revision as "optional" or confuse it with editing for conventions. This is a good time to bring in guest speakers who have had writing published. (They may even be former students!) The authors will, no doubt, discuss how much revision was necessary before their work was as good as it could be.

Minilessons on editing may surprise the candidates. They are used to having instructors mark all their errors on a draft so that they can copy the corrections on their final paper. But no more! The responsibility for the quality of writing is directed away from the instructor and back to the writer. The goal is to satisfy the intended audience, not just the instructor. Candidates learn to use resources like a writing handbook, a thesaurus, the dictionary, the college/university writing center, and to ask a "knowledgeable other" (which could be the instructor, but not necessarily) specific questions. The candidate, not the instructor, is the editor.

The final minilessons of the semester instruct candidates how to prepare pieces of writing for publication. Publication is defined as getting writing out of the classroom. Typical publications include submitting poetry, essays, stories, or articles to magazines, newspapers, online publishers, or contests. More ideas are included later in the chapter under Publishing.

The minilesson is the teacher-directed portion of writing workshop, although an instructor's choice of a lesson is always in response to writers' needs. It is also appropriate to end the writing workshop with a 2-3 minute minilesson that sends candidates off with a thought to ponder or a task to complete, such as asking them to pay attention to conversations they participate in during the next week because the next minilesson will address how to write dialogue.

INDEPENDENT WRITING

After the minilesson, candidates have time to write on topics of their own choice. Some choose to stay in class to write in notebooks or on laptops, others prefer the computer lab, and still others visit the library to read and do research for their pieces. The instructor uses this time to write as time permits, preparing pieces that she will share with candidates as the semester progresses.

This time is also used for candidate-instructor conferences. A schedule ensures that each candidate meets with the instructor several times throughout the semester. In addition, candidates are encouraged to come with questions or pressing needs during this time. The instructor serves as a knowledgeable other regarding all writing issues.

Independent writing time may last 15 minutes or an hour, depending on the length of the class. If your class meets once a week for two hours or more, you may want to have a minilesson, writing time, a break, another minilesson, and continued writing time. Sometimes the second minilesson is led by a candidate who has experience or expertise in a particular area related to writing. The important thing is that candidates are given time in class to write. Candidates grasp that writing is important when the instructor devotes class time to it.

PEER CONFERENCING

After writing time is completed, candidates spend some time sharing their writing with each other. Consider that each class's personality is different when organizing the sharing time. For example, some candidates like to choose their own groups and share with different classmates each time. Other times, class members are reluctant and it is better for the instructor to form sharing pairs or small groups. Sharing groups may stay the same for the semester or they may change as the need arises.

The most important characteristic of sharing time is that candidates feel comfortable enough to risk sharing their writing with others. They need to learn to trust their group so that they can truly help each other work with their writing. All groups will feel tentative at first. Trust takes time to build, *but when it happens, writing achievement soars*.

At first, groups usually talk about their writing topics with each other. Progress is made when they begin to read sections of their writing to each other or trade papers to read silently. Comments will be exclusively positive at first, but as the group grows together as writers, more forthright comments will be common. When a group becomes confident and successful; ask them to share their experiences and techniques with the rest of the class.

Peer conferencing sheets that candidates prepare before meeting with their partners or groups are a useful starting point for the conversation. When candidates naturally begin to conference effectively, they won't need them anymore and they can be abandoned. (See Appendix A for a sample peer conferencing sheet.)

PUBLISHING

A key piece of writing workshop is publishing; to share writing outside the classroom. When we extend the opportunity to publish to our candidates, it ignites their passion to write because it provides authenticity and meaning to their work. The instructor will provide some venues for publication but will also send candidates to search for publication opportunities to share with the class. Students will start to notice postings about poetry readings, short story contests, and opportunities to respond to an editorial in the local newspaper. Online publishers change almost daily, and as technology advances, so do the possibilities to share writing.

Examples of publications include the following:

- letters to servicemen and women stationed overseas
- picture books shared with a classroom of young children
- poetry framed and given as a gift
- original songs recorded on a CD
- speeches for a scholarship competition
- continuous online blogs
- a class anthology of poetry and essays edited by a student in the course
- letters from a father to his newborn daughter

Venues for writing are limitless and will change each semester depending on candidate interests, experiences, and areas of expertise.

READING AND WRITING GOALS

Every course has certain requirements that candidates need to accomplish to receive college credit. For example, I require that four writing pieces are taken to publication, including one of length (a short story, novel chapter, nonfiction article, etc.). But candidates also have the opportunity to decide on their own reading and writing goals, which count toward their grades as well.

Candidates set four personal *writing* goals. These often address genre ("I want to try to write free verse poetry"), but other types of goals include spending more time on revision, keeping a daily record of writing ideas, or visiting the college writing center regularly to get help with editing.

Since reading informs writing, candidates must read at least 800 pages of their choice. Everything counts except reading for another course (no double dipping!). That's the instructor's requirement. Candidates also set three *reading* goals of their own choosing. For instance, their goals can relate to genres (reading more poetry), to reading habits (reading each night before bed), or to improving reading (increasing reading speed).

At the end of the course, candidates present evidence of their goal achievement and write a reflection that includes a discussion of how they met their goals. Setting and achieving personal goals encourages an intrinsic motivation to write that will carry over to the candidates' teaching of writing someday.

ASSESSMENT OF CANDIDATE WRITING

Both formative and summative assessment is important in writing workshop. Each happens in a variety of ways as writing workshop progresses.

Formative assessment occurs during instructor-candidate conferences when the instructor takes notes to refer back to when gauging progress. Checks of rough draft writing, the Idea Book, and progress on goals happen regularly. Peer conferences are assessed by tracking meeting times and evaluating the quality of completed peer conferencing sheets. The instructor also meets with each peer group regularly to discuss their progress, answer questions, and address needs.

Rubrics are developed to help in the assessment process. Establishing rubrics that candidates see before beginning writing workshop, and then see again as evidence of their grade, are most effective. (See Appendix B for a sample rubric for the Idea Book.)

Summative assessments are given on completed goals and published pieces. Goals should show evidence of achievement and then are used to inform the setting of new goals. Published pieces are expected to conform to standard grammar, spelling, and structure requirements, as well as demonstrate risk-taking, depth and breadth of genre and writing style, and evidence of publication in appropriate venues. Candidates also write a summative reflection on their progress to demonstrate how they used the various course products to improve their writing.

AUTHORS' TEA

Writing can be a pleasurable, satisfying, profoundly meaningful activity and should be celebrated. At the end of each semester, the writing workshop class gathers for their final exam: to eat some treats and share their favorite pieces. Revision and editing are over. Peer conferences are completed. Writers' block is forgotten. All that is left is to enjoy. The candidates and the instructor sit in a large circle to laugh at the humorous pieces, cry at the poignant ones, and rejoice in the writing that's been achieved. It is a time to reflect on how writing workshop has changed writers and changed lives.

TEACHER CANDIDATES BECOME WRITERS

Through personal participation in writing workshop, candidates learn the importance and effectiveness of time, choice, ownership, and response for writing. The experience is a powerful teaching tool which proves to candidates that since writing workshop works for them, it is a viable framework for young students learning to write as well.

It is important that the instructor of the college classroom helps candidates see how writing workshop can fit into a robust classroom writing program alongside other writing activities required by the district or national standards. Writing workshop does not take the place of other kinds of writing instruction, but can augment the writing program by providing intrinsic motivation to write, interest in various types of writing, meaning in writing, and plentiful time to write.

Teacher beliefs are often the most influential aspect of decision-making in teaching. At the college where I teach, *Writing Across the Curriculum* is a required course for education majors, and its main goal is to change candidate beliefs about writing for themselves and being writing teachers. Extended participation in a writing workshop convinces candidates of its efficacy as a writing instruction tool for their future classrooms.

Changing the Meaning of Teacher Candidates' Experience with Writing

Over a period of ten semesters, teacher candidates in the writing workshop course titled, *Writing Across the Curriculum,* wrote reflections at the end of the course which described their growth as a writers. Portions of their reflective narratives are presented below to provide examples that their experience with writing had changed during the course.

Through content analysis, six categories were observed in the candidates' reflective narratives:

- Process
- Motivation to write
- Revision and editing
- Taking risks
- Conferencing
- Publishing

The following quotes from candidate reflections exemplify the experiences that candidates had that changed their beliefs about writing. They recount the "Aha" moments in their own writing, which prepares them to encourage and expect this from their own students as well. (All names are pseudonyms.)

Process

"At first I abandoned the paper but then eventually at the end of the semester I had more ideas that I kept adding to the piece" (Maura).

"I began writing a memoir about Dusty about a month ago. I had written a few rough drafts about him but none that really pleased me. Some of the rough drafts included how the accident happened ... I decided to write about who Dusty was and what kind of a person he was ... I felt this was the best writing I had done about him because it didn't talk about the accident, just him" (Aron).

"This process was challenging but enjoyable ... sometimes I got stuck and just had to put my pen down and think! Other times I had so many ideas that I didn't know when I would stop writing! I look forward to finishing this piece and giving it to my grandfather for Christmas. I think I'll even read (it) aloud to the whole family on Christmas day" (Suzanne).

"I gave up on the piece and almost forgot about it until I was reorganizing my folder. I saw the piece and noticed I could possibly make it a poem. There was not enough to make it a good story but too much to simply forget about it" (Carrie).

Motivation to Write

"Within this semester, I have written much more than I ever have before" (Michael).

"When we began this class I knew I would write about Grandpa" (Nickie).

"I never really sat down and told my brother how important he was in my life, and I don't think I would ever be able to have that type of conversation with him. So for this class, I thought it would be a perfect opportunity to sit down and write a letter to him" (Diane).

"Finding words to rhyme usually is hard for me, but somehow it was easy for me to find words that rhymed (this time). I think it was because I got to write about my favorite sport" (Ryan).

"This was such an emotional process (writing about her grandmother's death) but it felt so good to write an essay that had meaning" (Danielle).

Revision and Editing

"I revised and edited the poem at least six times before I was satisfied with the final piece. After completing the poem, I felt a sense of pride and accomplishment for the first time!" (Angel).

"What surprised me when I was done was how much extra time it took to make the poem sound nice, and it had me wonder how many rewrites it takes an actual poet to make their poems perfect" (Kevin).

"Before this class I would have never taken another glance after my first draft. Now I realize what makes a paper great is revising ... and not being afraid to take risks" (Carolann).

"In my second essay, I wrote with stronger vocabulary ... it made me wonder if it was because my mood was different or simply because I've grown as a writer" (Kaitlyn).

Taking Risks

"I started this (poem) by thinking about someone else's life and putting myself in their (sic) head ... someone I know who is addicted to alcohol. I wanted the poem to be scatterbrained and kind of schizophrenic in a way. I did not want it to be perfectly written. I also wanted the verse to show what happens when you drink. I did not expect this to go in depth or get as good as it did" (Ashley).

Conferencing

"I didn't know how to start the poem off. Then I had a talk with Antonio (a peer) and he told me to just write about my feelings. I let Antonio read it and he said it was okay but it could be better. He said I needed to express my feelings clearer and make it flow. After I reread it, he was right. So I revised it ... and when I was done I was proud of myself" (Mari).

"I had ... a lot of feedback from my group (peer conferencing group). I didn't always use what they suggested but often their opinions gave me new ideas..." (Corey).

Publishing

"I think that my family helped me feel that I have better writing skills because they were surprised that poem came from me" (Maria).

"One thing I wrote was a diary for my (future) children. I got the idea from a book I read ... The book inspired me to keep a diary about myself now so one day I will be able to share with my children the amazing things that had happened in my life" (Amy).

"I think the reason I like my memoir so much is because I had to take a risk to write it. That experience is held close to my heart, and it's not something I talk about often. I do want to publish it one day. I'm just not ready to share it with an audience just yet" (Martina).

In order to be change agents in the writing classroom, candidates need to undergo a personal change of beliefs that can undergird their classroom practice. The reflective narrative testimonies above express some of the heart and passion that occur during writing workshop and as witnessed by this professor. A course that implements writing workshop can be the event that changes a candidate's view of writing and how to teach it.

TEACHER CANDIDATES BECOME TEACHERS OF WRITING

Of course the ultimate goal of writing workshop in the college classroom is to impact the writing of K-12 students. Teachers who hold and practice beliefs and processes about writing such as those quoted above are ready to take them into the K-12 classroom. They are equipped to motivate their students to write, demonstrate successful writing processes, and provide meaningful publication outlets. As we often hear, a teacher of writing (and *all* teachers teach writing to some degree) needs to be *a teacher who writes* – not necessarily a published author or expert in the field, but someone who writes as part of life and shares this experience with students.

The same framework used in the college classroom – minilesson, independent writing of choice, conferencing, and sharing/publishing – can be used in the elementary or secondary classroom. Appendix C shows sample daily schedules to demonstrate how writing workshop can fit into writing programs already in place in the classroom. While writing workshop is not the only writing that happens in the classroom, it is, however, a vital component of an effective, rigorous writing program.

Writing workshop provides four things that the typical writing program on its own is lacking:

- First, it teaches students to peer conference, which taps into their need to construct knowledge socially.
- Second, it cements a reading-writing connection through the use of mentor texts and read alouds.
- Third, it provides outlets for publishing writing outside the classroom which demonstrates to students a purpose for revising and editing.
- Fourth, it inspires motivation through choice of topics and support of meaningful writing.

The bottom line is that no matter how engaging the writing prompt, how well-crafted the writing lesson, or how important the writing test, students will not reach today's high standards without teachers who have confidence in their own writing as well as the knowledge and desire to provide effective writing instruction in the classroom.

CONCLUSION

Returning to the question posed at the beginning of this chapter, the answer is yes, writing workshop is an effective, viable framework to teach students of all ages to be successful, motivated writers. However, writing workshop needs to be perceived not as simply another writing activity to squeeze into the daily routine of the classroom, but as a philosophical stance that permeates the classroom climate.

REFERENCES

Anderson, (2000). *How's it going?* Portsmouth, NH: Heinemann.
Atwell, N. (1987). *In the middle.* Portsmouth, NH: Heinemann.
Butler, A., & Turbill, J. (1987). *Towards a reading-writing classroom.* Portsmouth, NH: Heinemann.
Calkins, L.M. (1986). *The art of teaching writing.* Portsmouth, NH: Heinemann.
Cappello, M. (2010). Supporting independent writing: A continuum of writing instruction. In Marva Cappello & Barbara Moss (Eds.), *Contemporary readings in literacy education* (pp. 237-243). Los Angeles: Sage.
Graves, D. (1983). *Writing: Teachers and students at work.* Portsmouth, NH: Heinemann.
Harris, T.L., & Hodges, R.E. (1995). *The literacy dictionary.* Newark, DE: International Reading Association.
Heard, G. (1989). *For the good of the earth and the sun.* Portsmouth, NH: Heinemann.
National Commission of Writing in America's Schools and Colleges (2003). *The neglected "r": The need for a writing revolution.* College Entrance Examination Board.
Overmeyer, M. (2005). *When writing workshop isn't working.* Portland, ME: Stenhouse.
Smith, F. (1983). *Essays into literacy.* Portsmouth, NH: Heinemann.
Tompkins, G. (2006). *Literacy for the 21st century: A balanced approach.* Upper Saddle River, NJ: Pearson.
Weber, C. (2002). *Publishing with students.* Portsmouth, NH: Heinemann.
Whitney, A., Blau, S., Bright, A., Cabe, R., Dewar, T., Levin, J., Macias, R., & Rogers, P., (2010). Beyond strategies: Teacher practice, writing process, and the influence of inquiry. In Marva Cappello & Barbara Moss (Eds.), *Contemporary readings in literacy education* (pp. 245-264). Los Angeles: Sage.

APPENDIX A

Peer Conferencing Sheet
Please complete this sheet before meeting with your peer conferencing group.

1. How did you feel while you were writing today?
2. What was the strength of your writing?
3. What was a challenge? How can your group help you?

48   *Chapter 3*

4. Share a piece of your writing with your peer conferencing group. It may be the whole piece, a paragraph, or even one sentence. Discuss parts for celebration and ideas for revision.
5. What is your plan for the next class period?

The writer:

The conferencing group:

APPENDIX B

Table 3B.1 Assessment Rubric for the Idea Book

	1	2	3	4
Persistence	Ideas and topics for writing are noted sporadically with little organization or consistency.	Ideas and topics for writing are noted *almost* every day.	Ideas and topics for writing are noted *every* day.	Ideas and topics for writing are noted every day and go beyond the expected length and depth of entries.
Connections	Ideas and topics show little connection to personal experience, class experience, and/or readings.	Ideas and topics show some connection to personal experience, class experience, and/or readings.	Ideas and topics show insightful connections to personal experience, class experience, and readings.	Ideas and topics show insightful connections to personal experience, class experience, and readings. They go beyond the expected level of depth and originality.
Reflection	The Idea Notebook demonstrates sparse detail and is not descriptive or inventive.	The Idea Notebook demonstrates some detail and description.	The Idea Notebook demonstrates rich detail and description.	The Idea Notebook demonstrates rich detail and description, and a unique approach that represents the writer.

Scoring Key:

1=Unacceptable Evidence;
2=Limited Evidence;
3=Acceptable Evidence;
4=Exceptional Evidence

APPENDIX C

Sample Daily Schedules for Writing Workshop

Elementary School

8:00-8:20
Reading Workshop (self-selected reading; make connections between reading and writing)
8:20-8:30
Calendar and Word of the Day (vocabulary)
8:30-9:30
Guided Reading Groups/Literature Circles (reading and writing centers)
9:30-9:45 Recess
9:45-10:30
Writing Workshop (conferences)
10:30-11:00
Spelling, word study
11:00-11:30 Lunch
11:30-12:00
Shared Book Experience (books of various genres, including mentor texts for writing workshop and nonfiction related to math, science, social studies curriculum)
12:00-2:30
Science, social studies, math, specials, etc. (Remember to have students read and write in the content areas as well!)
2:30-2:45 Novel read aloud
2:50 Dismissal

Middle School/High School Language Arts

Daily meetings of 45 minutes

Monday

- Skills/strategies for the week (grammar, spelling, comprehension strategies, etc.)

Tuesday

- Reading Workshop
- 15 minute minilesson
- 20 minute reading time
- 10 minutes to share in small groups
- (response journals, book recommendations, literature circles)

Wednesday through Friday

- Writing Workshop
- 15 minute minilesson
- 25 minutes writing time with conferences (publishing, sharing)
- 5 minutes for closure

Block Scheduling – 90 minute periods
Independent reading of choice – 20 minutes
Reading and/or writing minilesson – 20 minutes
Time to read/write – 35 minutes
Time to conference/share/publish – 15 minutes

Turning Point: The Spelling Test

Paula P. Daniels, First-Grade Teacher

It was time for Friday's spelling test. All the students hesitantly readied their papers and pencils and I began to read off the list of words. My mind wandered as I said the words, knowing exactly which students would miss most of the words and which students would ace the test. No matter how many spelling worksheets we did, or how many spelling bees we had, the result was almost always the same. Most disturbing of all was that the words the students were spelling correctly on the test would be spelled incorrectly in their writing the next week.

I finally decided to take action. For several weeks, I kept diligent notes on the words in our spelling program that students spelled incorrectly in their writing after the test. It was as I thought; there seemed to be no correlation between spelling the words correctly on the test and spelling them correctly in the stories, reports, journals, and letters that students routinely wrote in class.

I took my research to the district reading/writing specialist and explained it to her at one of our training sessions. I also told her my plan for a different spelling program which included a word wall for use as a resource, frequent word sorting activities, a focus on the words that students used most often, and lots and lots and *lots* of reading and writing.

She said, "Go for it!" She thought the goals of my program actually aligned quite well with the district's goals for reading, writing, and spelling. One of my grade-level teammates also expressed interest in trying the program.

We implemented the program and our classes read and wrote throughout the day and across the curriculum. I collected more data. Were the students spelling words more accurately? I meticulously counted correct and incorrect words in all of their writing. I expected good things from the research, but the results surprised even me. Near the end of the school year, even my students' state test scores in writing were higher than the previous year.

My reading/writing specialist was thrilled. "Keep going!" she said.

Suddenly the word spread that my students did not take spelling tests. The teacher next door to me asked where our spelling books were. The teacher down the hall wanted to know what words my students were studying.

Happily, I explained my new approach. The teachers nodded and went on their way. I guessed they weren't too impressed until the following year when I heard that more and more teachers decided to do away with the weekly spelling tests. They embraced working with words through the use of writing journals and even began using the journals to look at their students' spelling to determine words to study!

I felt great. I'd made a change in my school that benefited students and teachers. Students were truly learning to spell.

My spelling program had passed the test!

Chapter Four

Crafting Inquiry in the Preservice Classroom: Tensions and Possibilities

Leah T. Lembo

The methods semester in a teacher education program is a pinnacle experience for those preparing to become classroom teachers. It has the potential to help students connect learning gleaned through readings, discussions, and written assignments completed during previous coursework, with the application of this material in the field. Many schools of education struggle to balance the equation between field experience and related coursework in order to provide the best configuration of circumstances for students who undertake this intensive semester of preparation.

Professors in methods classrooms attempt to guide students in building connective bridges between theory and practice. While the bridge building metaphor suggests something technical and concrete, the actual process of helping teacher candidates to connect theory with practice is much more abstract.

As professors in education, we are charged not only with this sometimes daunting task, but with nurturing the passions of aspiring teachers as they begin to confront what are sometimes adverse experiences in public school classrooms. The practices they see are often normative and may conflict with ideas espoused by education professors they have studied under. This is particularly true in education departments which adhere to a constructivist framework or for the many more that have leanings in this direction.

A CONSTRUCTIVIST METHODS CLASSROOM

Using a constructivist framework, teacher candidates are taught to view learning as something more than the mere transmission of information from teacher to student. They are encouraged to understand the need for deep content knowledge coupled with the skills of good facilitation. Within this context, the importance of social collaboration and peer to peer interaction in the learning process is emphasized.

In methods courses, teacher candidates learn about project-based curriculum, thematic units, and inquiry. They are taught to look past the traditional textbook approach and to use multiple resources, searching for various perspectives. They are asked to explore beyond the algorithm, demonstrate learning through performance, and to venture beyond the memorization of information.

As constructivists, we discourage perspectives that consider students empty vessels and emphasize the need to see each one as an individual with varying background experiences, interests, and inclinations. We view teaching as craft, art, and science; and learning as an integrative experience.

The dilemmas that face college professors and their teacher candidates in the intricate process described above are conceptual, cultural, political, and pedagogical (Windshitl, 2002). The exploration of one particular subject in this assembly, inquiry-based learning, touches upon all four dilemmas, as Windshitl describes them, and encompasses many other important issues. Using inquiry-based learning and implementation as a lens for this discussion, a number of the issues tackled by both students and educators in the methods classroom will be illuminated.

This chapter will focus on using inquiry in the preservice classroom. Some of the tensions associated with this process will be described in the first section and ways to counter them will be suggested through the description on inquiry-based learning that follows. The goal is to define the purposes of inquiry-based learning more broadly and to discuss its relevance to teaching diverse learners.

CONFRONTING THE TENSIONS

As we prepare students to move confidently through the transition towards leadership of their own classrooms, helping them to cultivate ownership over new methods is crucial. Using inquiry in the college classroom not only provides an ideal vehicle for understanding, but it allows us to confront the tensions while exploring the possibilities of this powerful model for teaching and learning.

Perhaps professors in other disciplines such as geology, art, or literature have a more straightforward charge, as they are responsible for teaching a single subject at one time. In teaching about teaching and learning (an area of study that is inherently multi-disciplinary in addition to being political and sometimes contentious), we often face barriers that are beyond our control as teacher-scholars in a society that is increasingly fraught by and driven in accord with public opinion.

Complicating our task further, schools play an integral role in children's development and are often mischaracterized, misunderstood, and even blamed for many of our shortcomings as a nation. Contemporary teacher education programs operate within a society that is often focused on what is easy, quick, and immediate. Influenced by constant change and technology, many have come to believe that anything can be easily fixed, including our schools.

Amidst this climate, education programs must provide strong foundations in theory, pedagogy, and content fused with related field experiences to prepare candidates for the complex careers they face as elementary classroom teachers. They will be expected to teach a wide range of school subjects while possessing a span of related abilities that support them in this process. There is nothing quick or easy about this progression and while we claim to "prepare" teachers, if we are brutally honest, we can admit that we have still barely scratched the surface after four years. The profession demands a great deal from those who choose to enter, and experience is one of its best teachers.

PREVIOUS EDUCATIONAL EXPERIENCE

In professional programs, we provide as many valuable experiences possible to teacher candidates, in and out of the college classroom. An education professor can present links between theory and practice and act as an important conduit for students by presenting seminal research and by modeling dispositions and methods for best practice.

However, the methods classroom has the potential to do more, and can offer students personal experiences that are illustrative of these theories and methods, though this is by no means a light hearted endeavor. The ways in which teacher candidates were educated before coming to college, the kind of educational experiences they have in conjunction with their required education coursework during college, and the societal norms that shape the firmament of our past and current educational landscape, all contribute to the tensions we face in preparing new teachers.

We must first seriously consider that most of our college students have not been taught under the auspices of the methods we encourage them to embrace and some may even feel affronted by these approaches. Many have an established impression of what it means to be a "good student" and it may be very different from our own, as academics and as learners.

For them, by and large, being a good student means getting good grades by doing the assigned work, completing homework, studying for the test, and getting the right answers. They may not have experienced an inquiry-based approach before, save a few brief encounters in high school science classes. Their recollection of doing projects in school may consist only of the most memorable shoebox diorama. And their success is not only self-affirmed; they have been likely extolled by teachers, parents, and the often underestimated commercial media.

Collectively, society has sent them a clear message, and many have bought it: if they get good grades they are well on their way to achieving the meritocratic American dream.

Despite this familiar backdrop, the academic's explanation of best practice and what it means to be successful in school is often quite different from many of educations' stakeholders' perspectives, beliefs, and well established conventions. A group that includes principals, parents, and experienced classroom teachers (among others), these stakeholders are most influential over the education landscape. As we enthusiastically prepare teacher candidates to delve into inquiry-based learning or other constructivist-based approaches, we unwittingly push them right into the epicenter of a debate that has raged for more than a century over progressive verses traditional education.

In a sense, we ask our teacher candidates to develop a blind idealism to inquiry or other methods, when in truth; they are not yet invested in them. They have yet to develop a sincere commitment to approaches that may be counterintuitive. Even if achieved, this kind of idealism is unlikely to be sustainable for these future teachers. We prepare them to act as pilots of their own craft but when they arrive they find that their crafts are being driven by something that more resembles a remote pilot. Once they are immersed in the traditional schools that hire them, many will be inducted into a world that is standards driven, externally monitored, and commercially published.

These conditions have the potential to abruptly uproot the foundations professors are so dedicated to cultivating in the college classroom. This makes *ownership* an essential component of any teacher training program. If students do not earnestly buy-in or feel a sense of ownership over this new and daring approach to learning, they are unlikely to practice it successfully or practice it at all. Inquiry-based learning pushes some of these students out of their comfort zones and asks them to reconsider their own norms, restructure their learning habits, and acquire new dispositions.

The affront begins when we challenge societal norms by telling our students that according to educational philosophy and learning theory, it is better to abandon the way they have "done school" for well over a decade, and to do it our way, or to consider Dewey's wisdom, Bruner's research, or Piaget's developmental stages. Tacitly we push the message that even if they consider themselves to be good students, if they believe that the education they have had was a good and successful one, or if they consider themselves to be smart or intelligent, we insist that there is more to schooling that they have either missed, or not yet encountered.

Societal norms are once again crossed when, in the course of studying to become a teacher, our candidates are asked to critically examine the role that testing plays in evaluating student progress, to think deeply about how the results of such tests inform, or should inform, instructional decisions and to consider how, or if at all, off the shelf tests measure the progress that both students and teachers make regularly. They are asked to understand and to consider multiple forms of evidence for learning, including performances, artwork, and portfolios, and taught to use student work products as tools to help them reflect on their instructional practices.

Students are also pressed to develop an informed understanding of the issues and policies that surround the testing movement. They need to acknowledge the reality that states, districts, and the federal government are increasingly focused on the use of tests, and in some cases, the merit based pay for teachers which rests upon their results.

Tangled with all of this, too, is the reality that our students themselves have taken and passed standardized tests. The SAT was probably a required gateway to college entrance, to their seats in our own classrooms; and the PRAXIS or other similar exams will provide access to their new careers in teaching. These dueling realities are ever present in our methods classrooms, and as we encourage students to understand the relative benefits of testing, we invite them to re-examine the norms and to consider that there are other, more effective ways to evaluate student learning.

CONTENT KNOWLEDGE

Another tension that arises in the methods classroom is related to one of inquiry's major prerequisites: content knowledge. As students undertake a professional program in education, they must work to satisfy the liberal arts or core curricular requirements for their Bachelor's degrees. These two strands occur in tandem and will inevitably and necessarily influence one another. In many cases, within the courses teacher candidates typically take, whether world geography, U.S. history or English literature, they are exposed to more traditional methods while doing so. Instructors tend to cover such topics very broadly forcing students to rely heavily on memorization of material that is likely to be easily forgotten.

This experience may send yet another mixed message about the purpose of learning, as it occurs in stark contrast to more constructivist approaches used in our education courses. These courses tend to be far less prescriptive and invite students to become deeply engaged in learning experiences that are more likely to inspire connections which can lead to enduring understandings. In this way, the other coursework can potentially run counter to our efforts and dampen the expectation that students will have acquired some solid content knowledge in the humanities and sciences that can be readily applied to courses which emphasize curriculum and pedagogy.

Students who come to us during the methods semester with little in-depth knowledge about history, geography or science, can face excruciating hurdles as they embark upon developing good instructional designs for their practice classrooms. In order to develop well designed, workable investigations for the inquiry-based classroom, and to facilitate them skillfully, it is imperative for the teacher to have a strong working knowledge of the subject's content. A seeming paradox attached to this issue is posed by the fact that assuming to know everything about a given subject is unrealistic and virtually unattainable.

Such a belief, that the teacher is the keeper of all truth, or has a stronghold on the information in any one discipline, is not only an antiquated one, it is also contradictory to another foundational tenet of constructivism: that knowledge and information continue to grow exponentially (Jacobs, 1989) and cannot be viewed as something static.

INTELLECTUAL CURIOSITY

Inquiry's other, and no less important prerequisite, is intellectual curiosity. It is crucial for teachers to be open-minded, always, and to consistently model the dispositions of inquiry by being curious, thoughtful, and willing to learn beside and along with their students, at any grade level. While it can easily be taken for granted in those who wish to become teachers, there is a significant difference between a desire to simply know a lot and get the answers, and genuine curiosity. The latter is typically characterized by an unyielding, inquisitive desire to understand things, often leaning towards the "how and why" of something rather than being satisfied solely by the "what."

Curiosity is an innate characteristic. Human beings are biologically predisposed to learning and children are especially ready to use their reasoning abilities to make sense of the world (Bransford, Brown & Cocking, 1999). In spite of this fact, experiences in school and at home can readily squelch this characteristic, rendering it inert in many people from very early ages. An over emphasis on the paradigm of right or wrong tends to heighten a desire to constantly be right.

Grant Wiggins (Wiggins & McTighe, 2005) reminds us of what is too often forgotten, that "understanding is not something binary . . . it is a matter of degree." But young learners soon find that people, including many of their teachers, only want to hear the perceived-to-be-correct answers and rarely dwell upon their misconceptions or less developed understandings. Even worse, the so called "wrong answers" may be disparaged and even uttering them out loud may be regarded as stupid or ridiculous by the adults who children so eagerly wish to emulate.

The debilitation of curiosity is not an uncommon phenomenon and presents yet another challenge for teacher education as we must revive and strengthen it in our teacher candidates before we can realistically expect them to nurture it in their own students one day.

HABITS OF MIND

Inquiry-based learning has the potential to develop a student's sense of wonderment and curiosity and can foster other characteristics that transfer to learning more generally. The dispositions for inquiry have forever been espoused by classical philosophers and more recently by Education's own John Dewey, but they are also well described in Costa & Kallick's series on the *Habits of Mind* (2000). Identified by these authors as sixteen characteristics, they include: persistence, flexible thinking, taking risks, questioning, and applying past knowledge to new situations, among many others.

Not unlike the fate of curiosity, the development of these traits has also been hampered by prevailing perspectives on what it means to be curious, or even what it means to be intelligent. Habits of mind go hand in hand with content knowledge, and in fact, such dispositions should be considered fuel for the acquisition of deep content knowledge. Yet teaching good dispositions directly or teaching them in isolation is not the best course of action.

It is not uncommon to find inservice teachers, motivated to improve their practice, search for formulas or recipes to teach these affective skills to their students, after being inspired by a workshop or because they were told that a new mandate has been launched in their district. Dispositions can be encouraged, but moreover they must be modeled within a context of mutual trust and mutual respect in a classroom community that honors and nurtures the uniqueness of every individual.

The inquiry-based methods classroom has the potential to be such an environment. Students are not only taught about inquiry-based methods, but taught through them. The acquisition of content knowledge can be facilitated; dispositions can be modeled and cultivated. Creating an inquiry-based methods classroom can provide teacher candidates with a viable model to build upon and can help them to gain the attitudes and to develop the convictions necessary to approach the conundrum of teaching inquiry within more traditionally bound school systems.

THE POSSIBILITIES OF INQUIRY-BASED LEARNING

"Questions can be more nurturing than answers." (Norman Mailer)

Many different constructivist-based formats have been developed for the classroom. Most notably among them are: project-based approaches, thematic units, interdisciplinary studies, problem-based learning, and inquiry. These approaches share many things in common and all offer points of departure from traditional textbook learning.

At base, each approach is conceived around a few common fundamental ideas that include involving students more actively in the learning process, emphasizing depth over breadth, and facilitating the often overlooked skills of *learning how to learn*. Many arguments have been posed about the definitions of each format, about the steps that should comprise them, and even more has been expounded on how they differ from each other. This ongoing disagreement represents a setback for progressive education, as it only pits allies against each other and helps to maintain education's persistent need to re-invent the wheel again and again.

It is possible that this ensuing argument over formats for learning may stem from the fact that implementation of any proposed idea can become different in practice and deviate drastically from the original premises upon which it was built. This happens with thematic curriculum often. Teachers sometimes use a theme as a conceptual hinge for a series of lessons, but continue to teach in superficial ways using instructional practices that look very similar to traditional whole group instruction.

This problem is one of implementation and inservice teacher training. It sometimes occurs due to school districts or principals who launch new initiatives with insufficient support for teachers, which may amount to little more than the introduction of new buzz words, short workshops, and more new requirements.

The simplification of any teaching method also happens because of individual dispositions, beliefs about teaching and learning, prior experiences, or because of the type of training, or lack thereof, teachers received before they began teaching. The opposite is also possible when a teacher takes an ordinary textbook and uses it well by including additional and varied source materials and providing new experiences for students that allow them to do extended classroom research on topics of interest covered with brevity in the textbook.

The problems associated with how teachers approach an idea in the classroom will always be as varied as people themselves. This underscores the importance of creating inquiry-based classrooms in education schools that give students firsthand experience with the methods in order to gain buy-in and an authentic understanding.

INQUIRY-BASED LEARNING IN PRACTICE

The remainder of this section provides an overview for inquiry-based learning and is intended for the methods instructor. There is little difference between presenting inquiry in the college classroom and the structure of such a project in a K-12 classroom thus a mirror effect is created in which education students are learning about an important method while learning *through* the method simultaneously. Making these mirror-like connections explicit throughout the semester may help students to understand both the practical and theoretical premises that ground inquiry in the classroom.

The ideas that lie beneath inquiry-based learning are as old as Socrates. Inquiry is often associated with science education, but by no means is it exclusive to this domain. The attribution is perhaps made because of a prevailing tradition in the science classroom that under the guise of "the scientific method" allows students to develop and test a hypothesis and sometimes perform hands on experiments.

This approach can provide students with an opportunity to understand the process of inquiry but it can easily become too formulaic and may fall short when it comes to helping students to develop the dispositions, knowledge, and skills needed for the acquisition of deeper understandings (Donovan & Bransford, 2005).

In short, the inquiry process includes the following components:

1. Questioning
2. Exploring and investigating
3. Describing and analyzing (constructing new knowledge)
4. Sharing with others

5. Reflecting on the process and the results
6. Asking a new question

Inquiry can be taught in any subject area, and at any grade level. The very notion of inquiry centers first on the idea of *questioning*. Students in traditional classrooms are most accustomed to being asked questions and being expected to answer them. While they readily pose questions of their own, they are often met with comments such as "good question," "interesting thought," or "maybe we will get back to that."

Teachers tend to focus on telling, rather than allowing students to discover. Bruner (1960) notes that classroom discussions and textbooks "talk about the conclusions [made by experts] in a field of inquiry rather than centering upon the inquiry itself" (p. 14).

In an inquiry-based approach to learning students' are encouraged to use questions to drive their own investigations. Learning is an active process in which students are allowed to make choices about what they want to learn, engage in constructive dialogues with teachers and other members of the class, gaining ownership in the learning process.

In an inquiry-based classroom the teacher becomes more of a facilitator rather than a dispenser of information. For teachers who fear "giving up" their job, it is important to note that this role is more complex than it sounds, and should not be treated lightly. In order to create the type of environment necessary for inquiry, and to provoke or inspire students to ask questions, two important conditions must initially be satisfied by the teacher:

1. Developing an atmosphere of trust and caring
2. Providing interesting subject matter

The first condition involves developing a classroom climate where collaboration replaces competition. This is essential. Students at any age come with pre-conceived notions about what it means to be intelligent and about how school works. But it is not difficult to motivate change as students can easily adapt to different perspectives when made explicit and if carefully modeled. The prevalent fear of being wrong must be faced and dealt with skillfully. The notion that a wrong answer is bad or unacceptable must be toppled. The fact that students' individual ideas, even if naïve in ways, are interesting, important, and can help lead to deeper understandings, should be the resounding message.

It is most important to convince students that there is more to learning, more to thinking, than to simply search for the correct answer. Modeling through meta-cognition provides a reliable vehicle for teachers when making this case. What most good thinkers usually do internally becomes a transparent process in the inquiry classroom. The teacher must thoughtfully demonstrate how to weigh information, by considering and dissecting different responses, and thinking through them aloud. By acknowledging the merits of an idea and respectfully casting aside its weaknesses, students may glimpse the processes which govern expert thinking.

The second necessary condition for inquiry-based learning is fertile and interesting subject matter. Using a rich generative theme as an overarching framework for the project's curriculum, a teacher can be sure that there will be something in it for everyone. It is important for the teacher to demonstrate knowledge and passion for the chosen theme and to help students find entry points, or a "way in" to connect with some of the inter-related ideas along the way.

There is an invisible question on every student's horizon and that is, "why does this matter to me?" Addressing this question openly, especially in the beginning of the investigation, will help students become more eager to enter the sometimes seemingly escteric domains we lead them through.

It is important to keep in mind that any given curriculum can be the framework for an inquiry project and that state and national curriculum standards do not conflict with or pose a threat with inquiry or other constructivist based formats. While open-ended activities tend to be characteristically part of an inquiry project, the need for objectives, learning outcomes, or content standards is not negated as a good inquiry-based investigation but is built upon all three. Open ended, in this sense, does not mean that there are no goals, but refers to the way in which students are *guided towards* the outcomes.

With the realization that learning is more a process than a formula, a skilled facilitator leads every student through an investigation by providing opportunities for varied experiences that ensure all learning styles have been considered. Gardner's (1993) theory of multiple intelligences forms the backdrop for this type of learning environment and should inform the facilitator's work. His theory reminds us that not only do people learn differently, but that intelligence is manifest in many ways.

In the case of a methods classroom, Gardner's work can be directly pointed to and explored through reading and discussion in conjunction with other course projects. In this way an obvious bridge between theory and practice is built.

Themes

In reference to beginning with fertile subject matter, the issue of what constitutes a theme versus a topic, and which one is better, more appropriate, or more *correct* has been grounds for much discussion. This is more a semantic argument than a conceptual debate. A generative theme is simply one that can generate many ideas, theories, or concepts.

Criteria for selecting good themes should rest upon their relevance to a given school's curriculum, the concerns or culture of its community, or the interests of students and teachers.

The chosen theme should have the potential to generate interesting questions and discussions; it may be one of social relevance, historical value, or intrinsic interest.

The theme may begin with something complex such as "the end of the cold war," or something seemingly general like "trees." Either of these can be qualified further, for example; life in Berlin after the Wall came down, or the disappearance of trees in the Amazon rainforests. A region or country can be used as a generative theme, but to avoid the stereotypic tourist approach to studying another culture, it is necessary to go beyond the encyclopedia in order to find out more about how it can be used to frame an interesting study.

If a class is learning about the Middle East, using Jordan as a theme may be viable. Expand this to "Jordan and its borders" and you get a very fertile topic that not only explores one country but allows students to understand the inter-dynamics which characterize a complex region. The most effective generative themes usually relate to topics from K-12 social studies or science curricula, but they may also be drawn more broadly from the arts (Leonardo's Renaissance) or humanities.

Another and somewhat different approach to inquiry involves using a concept as a generative theme, such as "peace" or "community." Erickson's (2002) work on concept-based curriculum is a definitive source for this approach which poses different challenges for teachers and students. The two approaches are almost inverted images of each other.

By using the first theme-based approach, students are guided in the process of starting big and eventually narrowing down, following the path that real research often takes. Using "the disappearance of trees in the Amazon rainforest" as a theme, students are invited to look for connections between what is happening to one habitat and what is also happening in others. They may come away understanding that there are rainforests with similar threats in other parts of the world.

Using the rainforest as a lens, learning can spread across the domains of ecology, endangered species, global interdependence, commerce, and economics as well as cultural oppression. Students eventually identify specific questions of interest to guide their investigations such as "How does destruction of the rainforests affect cancer research?" This seemingly narrow question can open the gates to information and experience that ultimately leads to insights and a deeper understanding of the theme's big ideas.

On the contrary, when using a concept as the foundation for a study, connections to concrete examples can be drawn in a myriad of ways. This can change the dynamic of the course and the types of understandings students come away with may be much broader. The model in this chapter is centered on theme-based curriculum.

THE LEARNING ENVIRONMENT

The methods employed during an inquiry-based investigation can create a learning landscape that begins to dismantle some of the factory model structures of a traditional classroom. While these ideas have caught on in many K-12 classrooms, college professors are still often confronted with long rows of individual desks in many of their lecture style classrooms. Teachers usually find that rows of student desks with the teacher's at the forefront may not be the best arrangement.

The physical configuration of a room can suggest much about the desired experiences and potential learning outcomes. Arranging the furniture with flexible groupings and keeping the format varied can influence the inter-dynamics and prevent too much routine from extinguishing excitement. Different physical arrangements provide better opportunities for paired or small group instruction, reading circles, exhibition arenas, or discussion forums. Resources should be made readily accessible to students, shifting the power that is usually held firmly by the teacher.

Contrary to the popular myth that "teachers never teach" in an inquiry classroom, it is important to emphasize that this type of learning is *least* effective in an atmosphere that lacks academic structures and teacher input. An inquiry project has specific conditions and boundaries that must be determined and regulated by the teacher constantly. The format can and absolutely should include some teacher telling.

The difference between teacher telling in traditional and inquiry-based classrooms is really one of purpose. The teacher lectures should not take away from the discovery process, but should serve to underscore findings, embellish understandings, provide points of clarification, or illuminate necessary content knowledge that the entire group can benefit from. Requisite for the teacher-facilitator in this role is a strong command of the subject matter but a still *percolating* curiosity about it.

In this way, the passion of a true lifelong learner comes through. This type of modeling also contributes to establishing a collaborative learning community and helps students to feel safe about sharing their own thoughts and discoveries.

Social Collaboration

The course of an investigation should depart from whole group activities to time for individual work and small group instruction, and to invite social collaboration or peer to peer interactions. It may begin with the group viewing and discussing an important film (sometimes with built in stopping points), reading an introductory text that raises good questions about the theme, taking a field visit, inviting in a guest speaker, or doing a creative activity that generates excitement.

Any of these components can be interspersed as the study unfolds, and can be foundation posts that enable students to connect their various topics of personal interest back to the larger whole. These experiences enable students to develop the needed content knowledge to understand the theme's intricacies on a deeper level.

The other decisive Socratic notion that lies beneath the inquiry process is *dialogue*. The investigations that take place in an inquiry-based classroom are dependent on it. Using an inquiry format in any classroom is not linear and requires meticulous flexibility on the part of teacher and students. While learning objectives, outcomes, and standards may rest underneath the curriculum, the process that drives it must be a *reflexive* one, in which teachers and students engage collaboratively in the process of knowledge construction.

A skilled facilitator carefully leads the group as they explore and review various source materials related to the generative theme broadly. Students are met with useful academic structures and inputs that help them as they carefully weigh ideas and information from multiple perspectives. Eventually students identify specific topics of intrigue and generate the personal questions that drive their own portions of the investigation further.

In the role of facilitator, the teacher helps students to evaluate new information, consider various viewpoints, and build new frameworks for understanding as they continue to explore the given theme by dismantling it and identifying smaller sub-topics using a variety of resources. She may offer students assurance that the course being followed is a productive one, or prompt them in other directions. If an established norm includes regular ongoing dialogue among class members in an atmosphere that permits risk taking and freedom of expression to flourish, it is easy and natural for the teacher to introduce new ideas or to recommend particular source material.

The chosen resources are critical to an investigation and students must take the time needed to review them carefully. In this way the infamous hunt and peck approach to learning is discouraged as students do not merely search for answers to pre-determined questions, they explore content with an open mind and generate questions of their own.

The selected resources may include, but are not limited to the following:

- primary source documents
- published articles
- adult-level books
- children's literature
- films
- music
- art
- field visits
- interviews
- artifacts

Such a collection of rich source materials will seed the ground for good discussions and enrich students' knowledge bases supporting them as they formulate opinions, evaluate theories, and synthesize ideas and information.

Peer to peer or student dialogue can be fostered in many ways including the use of *warm and cool* discussion groups for sharing. Both are intended to generate good discussion that helps to drive the investigations further.

This kind of social collaboration can inspire and prod individual's queries by fostering the evaluation of information and the development of new ideas. In a warm sharing group, students meet with others whose topics have strong connections with (or some relationship to) their own (for example, how does the disappearance of trees affect cancer research? and, how does a shaman learn to gather medicines in the rainforest?). In a cool sharing group the interests students are pursuing have less in common (for example, what happens to an animal that loses its habitat? and, how does a rainforest make rain?)

In both groups, students report on what they are learning, while exploring others' learning so that interesting exchanges can take place. Such exchanges not only help to spur the investigation further but help students to form connections with the big ideas that most likely serve as at the basis for the study's objectives and learning outcomes.

The facilitator can decide when and how to use warm and cool groups as a study unfolds. Much of this depends upon the particular groups that develop in a given class and how similar or different they are. The benefit of cool group sharing is being able to present information to an audience that may offer good questions from a fresh perspective. In a warm group the topics may resonate more with others and students may be able to offer each other advice and suggestions for resources.

ORGANIZATIONAL TOOLS

In order to help students track and make sense of ideas and information, different graphic organizational tools may be developed throughout the investigation. Concept maps with hierarchical structures are common to science while *inquiry maps* are more useful in capturing the multiplicity inherent in social studies. There is no one way to create such a heuristic device. Deciding how and when to ask students to create such maps must be determined by the teacher and should be done in advance. More important than the type of map itself is the clarity with which the teacher presents its proposed structure and purpose.

An inquiry map for a social studies related topic usually asks students to document several layers of learning underneath the larger generative theme guiding the study. These include sub-topics, and *sub* sub-topics, questions about the smaller topics, and eventually, a list of big ideas or essential understandings that capture the theme as a whole. The questions themselves drive the investigation. As a student pursues answers to these self-generated queries, they embark upon a learning journey that fleshes out the map further. An inquiry map may be embellished with directional arrows, extensions, or captions to depict the activity among its related elements.

Teaching time honored approaches to research methods occurs naturally in inquiry-based learning. In the college classroom it is important to make this process transparent and to emphasize the need for teacher candidates to transfer this to their own classrooms, invoking the mirror-effect once again.

It is often taken for granted that students at any age are proficient in using indexes, search engines, keywords, or simply "digging" for information. All of them are susceptible to developing facile tendencies driven by the information age and its alluringly quick answers. Inquiry takes the mind away from this and asks them to indulge with all five senses in a rich and varied exploration that requires time and patience.

While the internet can be a powerful tool for information gathering, it must not become "inquiry in a box" and supplant the process of what Sizer (1984) calls "using the mind well." Boundaries and explicit directives must be included for the procurement and use of resources during an inquiry project.

Assessment

As students begin to exhibit expert knowledge about the topics they have been investigating, the possibilities for assessments that demonstrate learning are endless. Both formative and summative assessments can take many forms including the following:

- oral presentations
- graphs
- diagrams and tables
- written reports
- letters or diaries
- artwork
- posters
- community projects
- songs or plays

Also, this list is not intended to exclude tests or quizzes devised by the teacher in conjunction with learning objectives set for the course.

Building bridges in the methods classroom between inquiry-based learning and the type of teaching we want teacher candidates to practice in their field placements classrooms simultaneously is always challenging. Teacher candidates are often asked to develop lessons or mini-units for their classrooms based on content being covered by their teachers or required by the school's curriculum. It may seem frustrating to ask methods students to conduct investigations about the Amazon Rainforest while they are being asked to create lessons about the Boston Tea Party.

The hope is that by engaging in rigorous selection and review of good resources for learning, social collaboration, and all of the other components of inquiry discussed here, that this learning and its respective methods will transfer to the instructional plans they are asked to develop. It is also entirely possible to select generative themes that arch over many of the topics that are likely to be encountered in the practice classrooms such as Slavery and Reconstruction, Abolition and the Underground Railroad, Westward Expansion, or many, many others from social studies or science.

The bridge building that occurs throughout the methods semester should be as seamless as it is explicit. The experiences offered must be authentic ones. Methods students should be invited to take off their hats as practice teachers and indulge as learners in investigations that stimulate their own intellectual curiosity. Without experience around questions and dialogue, they may easily fall back upon the many teacher's guides that fill their classroom shelves only to embark upon the dry, didactic teaching that offers little to young learners as they explore the world for the first time under our guidance.

CONCLUSION: TEACHING DIVERSE LEARNERS IN THE 21ST CENTURY

Students in today's public school classrooms represent one of the most diverse groups ever in the country's history. Demographic projections tell us that eventually the majority population in the United States will be in the minority. Classrooms in the 21st century come with different needs and pose new challenges in comparison with the ones that we and our students were once accustomed to. This contemporary issue is one of many that face upcoming teachers and is relevant to inquiry-based learning.

This chapter surveyed some of the tensions associated with teaching inquiry in the methods classroom and explored some of the exciting possibilities inquiry presents for learning. It is not only important for teacher candidates to gain firsthand experience with these methods but to grapple with some of the important pedagogical and social issues that surround them. It is valuable for students to think about the ways in which inquiry-based learning might address the needs of diverse learners and correlate with the demands of contemporary society.

In order to build these bridges between theory and practice in the methods classroom, good discussions should accompany the inquiry-based investigations. Discussions should openly examine inquiry's main tenets, including the importance of questioning, dialogue, content knowledge, and intellectual curiosity.

Classroom conversation should also examine the goals of inquiry-based learning explicitly. Inquiry presents a format that asks students to consider varied interpretations. It requires active participation and encourages ownership over passive receptivity. Inquiry involves taking risks, thinking critically and creatively, and being able to solve problems using a variety of approaches.

In the methods classroom, we counter notions about good schooling surreptitiously, again and again. Along the way we try carefully to avoid offending by not insulting where our students have been, or attempting to conquer the battle of the infamous either-or in the great education debate.

While inquiry-based learning may not be second nature to many traditionally educated students, many find it fresh and invigorating. Teaching about inquiry is not routinely met with resistance. In any given group there will always be a mixed reaction in process and outcome. This situation forces us to consider that many students have been underserved by traditional methods while others have been happy and/or seemingly successful.

This dichotomy also provides grounds for good discussion about the need to employ a variety of methods in the classroom, and may possibly deflect the glaring debate between traditional and progressive education.

The many threads which bind our discussions together should always be clearly exposed, and the goal itself should also remain explicit. With experience and enduring conviction we present something that has proven potential to change the learning landscape for many. Inquiry-based learning is a format that can release untapped potential in thousands of students, address diversity, and create the drive and the mechanisms that foster critical and creative thinking, problem solving, and lifelong learning.

Unless our undergraduates are able to develop the kind of ownership that we encourage them to foster in their own students one day, they will come away with ideas that are ephemeral and can easily slip away once the curriculum mandates and managers find their way in.

Foundational readings and academic discussions may help to inform students about inquiry-based learning in the college classroom, but they cannot supplant authentic learning experiences. To remain faithful to the theories that we teach, it is important to offer students the chance to learn directly through these methods. Through this difficult and important work, we are tearing down the infrastructures from the industrial revolution's factory model school system and attempting to rebuild one for the knowledge society of the 21st century.

REFERENCES

Bransford, J. D., Brown, A.L., & Cocking, R.R. (Ed.). (1999). *How people learn: Brain, mind experience, and school*. Washington, D.C.: National Academy Press.

Bruner, J. (1960). *The process of education*. MA: Harvard University Press.

Donovan, M.S., & Bransford, J. (Ed.). (2005). *How students learn: History, math and science in the classroom*. Washington, D.C.: National Academy Press.

Costa, A.L., & Kallick, B. (2000). *Activating and engaging habits of mind*. VA: Association for Supervision and Curriculum Development.

Erickson, L, H. (2002). *Concept-based curriculum and instruction: Teaching beyond the facts*. Thousand Oaks, California: Corwin Press.

Gardner, H. (1993) *Frames of mind: The theory of multiple intelligences*. NY: Basic Books.

Jacobs, H. (1989) *Interdisciplinary curriculum: Design and implementation*. VA: Association for Supervision and Curriculum Development.

Sizer, T. (1984). *Horace's Compromise: The dilemma of the American high school*. Boston: Houghton Mifflin.

Wiggins, G., & McTighe, J. (2005). *Understanding by design*. VA: Association for Supervision and curriculum Development.

Windshitl, M. (2002). Framing constructivism in practice as the negotiation of dilemmas: An analysis of the conceptual, pedagogical, cultural, and political challenges facing teachers. *Review of Educational Research, 72, (2),* 131-175.

Turning Point: Change of Plans

Patti L. Sandy, 1st Grade Teacher

My Monday morning began with nineteen first graders bursting through the classroom door to tell me about the earthquake and tsunami that had just occurred in Japan. Everyone was talking at once as we shared our shock and our tears.

I encouraged the students to get paper and record their feelings and questions about the devastation in Japan. Our class calls it *"Hot News Right Off The Press."* At calendar time, students took turns sharing their *Hot News* while sitting in the author's chair. Miss Bailey, the teacher candidate placed in my classroom for the semester, sat quietly observing from the back of the room.

In the two months she had been with us, I had noticed how soft spoken and shy she was, comfortable with small groups of students but never addressing the whole class. That morning, the students had many comments and questions about how an earthquake and tsunami form.

As I carefully led the class discussion on this horrific event, Miss Bailey volunteered an answer to one of the student's questions, prompting more questions and discussion. As the exchange unfolded, I noticed Miss Bailey inching further to the front of the classroom until she was right next to me and we found ourselves leading the discussion together.

Recognizing the significance of her transformation, I slowly withdrew from the exchange until she was leading it entirely. The students were so interested that when it was time for reading groups, we changed the planned material and quickly located books on earthquakes to use that day instead. As Miss Bailey tapped into the first graders' knowledge and extended it by introducing additional facts, I could see a new confidence in her.

Later that day, I received a phone call from Miss Bailey, asking if she could prepare a lesson on earthquakes and tsunamis to present to the class. I agreed at once and was delighted when, the next day, she came prepared with an engaging, well-researched lesson. We ended up using the Smart Board in the adjacent first grade classroom and Miss Bailey presented the lesson to the combined first-grade classes.

I could scarcely believe that this was the same reticent teacher candidate of only two days before. Since then, Miss Bailey has blossomed in the classroom, with the self-confidence to engage the entire class as readily as she would a small group or an individual student. I wondered what it was that made the difference in her. I think it was in her all along, waiting for the connections to be made between her knowledge and her experiences.

I've seen the awe and excitement in friends' faces when they tell of seeing an American eagle in the wild or dolphins swimming along the seashore. But this was so much more. I literally saw a teacher candidate break free of her cocoon and stretch her wings until she was strong enough to fly. I was actually present when Miss Bailey became a teacher.

Chapter Five

Changing Preservice Teachers' Perceptions of Science and Science Teaching through Guided Nature Journaling

B. Patricia Patterson

This chapter describes an instructional approach that has been successful in changing elementary teacher candidates' attitudes toward science and science teaching. In a course titled "Inquiry," candidates learn to *do* science, guided by an instructor in the role of knowledgeable other.

The major course activity requires participants to develop a personal nature journal. Participants learn to observe and describe objects, events, and interactions in familiar natural settings. Participants are guided to develop their journals into rich observational records using multiple perspectives and representational strategies. Journals become a personal record of the natural world and a data-rich source for engaging in scientific inquiry to learn science content.

The Guided Nature Journal is an instructional approach developed from an ongoing cycle of design-based research in a required junior level Inquiry course for teacher candidates in a traditional four year undergraduate initial preparation program. The research, developed in response to initial analyses of candidates' knowledge of science, targets the development and testing of efficient and impactful instructional methodologies that builds elementary teacher candidates' capacity for constructivist science teaching and improved scientific literacy.

As with all research, the instructional strategies, products, and assessments of the Guided Nature Journal are being continually refined through analysis and reflection after each instructional application. Over time sustained evidence has demonstrated the power of the model for accomplishing the stated instructional goals for scientific literacy among elementary teacher candidates. Examples of teacher work in the course and student work from teachers' classrooms provide evidence of the impact and transferability of the Guided Nature Journal for promoting scientific literacy, a major "change agent" goal for the science educator.

The steps of the approach and how journals are assessed is described in depth to encourage replication, modification, and communication from other teacher educators who might wish to use a similar approach to accomplish the same goals.

SCIENTIFIC LITERACY

The goal of national and state science standards is to create scientifically literate people.

Scientifically literate people know the origins, explanatory power, and limits of major scientific theories. Scientifically literate people know how and why scientific knowledge changes. Scientifically literate people view science as a universal human knowledge-making endeavor, rather than the exclusive domain of a "professional" scientist.

To become scientifically literate, learners should be guided to engage in the processes of inquiry, with the instructional goal of constructing authentic personal knowledge of major scientific concepts, principles and theories.

These principles of scientific literacy from the national science standards fall under the umbrella of the constructivist paradigm of learning which holds that all meaningful learning (that which is remembered and used in other contexts) is based in experience. It follows that under both constructivism and the principles of scientific literacy people become scientifically literate by doing science; and that science knowledge emerges from their experiences with the natural world.

The goal of the science educator is to create teachers who can help their students become scientifically literate people.

INQUIRY: THE KNOWLEDGE-MAKING PROCESS IN SCIENCE

Scientific knowledge is explanatory knowledge about systems in the natural world that is generated through the ongoing process of inquiry. As with the declarative knowledge in any discipline, scientific knowledge is organized hierarchically, from inclusive theory downward to specific fact. The structure was created and is continually evolving through the empirical process of inquiry.

Scientific inquiry is a broadly applicable stepwise thinking process grounded in empirical observation of structures, events and relationships in the natural world. When observations are of sufficient depth and breadth, they can be analyzed for regularities and interpreted to create general explanations that can be tested for their limits.

For example, an observable fact is that squirrels live in trees. Recognizing that many living things may be found in specific locations, led to the formation of the concept "habitat." Noticing that many organisms possess structures and behaviors that allow them to survive in a particular habitat led to the formation of the concept of "adaptation."

Defining the relationship between "habitat" and "adaptation" led to formation of the principle of competitive exclusion. Situating the principle of competitive exclusion into a larger context leads to the formation of theories, which are principles with even greater explanatory power. In the case of this example, the theory is natural selection, which explains not only the principle of competitive exclusion but also posits a mechanism for the diversity we observe among living things.

CHILDREN AS SCIENTISTS: TEACHERS AS NON-SCIENTISTS

Experience and research point out the fact that children are by nature curious about the natural world. Young children are pre-disposed to ask questions and learn how to find the answers themselves. A Vygotskyian approach to teaching, where a *knowledgeable other* guides the learner's thinking and supplies criteria by which the learner can evaluate their thinking is a natural fit for the way that young children want to learn.

However, uncertainty about science prevents many elementary teachers from going beyond the bare bones of a prescribed science curriculum in their classrooms. Thus the cycle of "learning science second-hand" is perpetuated at the outset of a child's formal schooling.

Eventually, children become disconnected from the idea that they can learn about the natural world on their own, much less comprehend what others know about the natural world, or how they have come to know this. As children become less concrete in their thinking and are expected to learn in the abstract, the lack of concrete experiences with the doing of science in their early years will further the disconnect between the theories of science they learn and their own experiences with the natural world.

There will be no experiential base of "doing" science from which to build knowledge of how theories in science are developed, or what situations in nature the theories explain. Children who have not experienced the doing of science could, and probably do, lose their potential to appreciate or understand the elegance of a well formed explanatory theory in science.

Most elementary instructional time is spent (and often mandated to be spent) on reading and mathematics. Teachers have little knowledge of how science could be meaningfully integrated into these two activities. Nor do they have the desire to explore such options if they have not had the meaning of their experiences with science changed.

Research has repeatedly shown that elementary teachers are content with delivery of a stunted and disconnected science curriculum. Science is usually squeezed into the week in alternation with social studies; and though often activity based and targeting "discovery," the activities have little purpose to either the students or the teacher because the teacher has no ownership of the content nor understands how the activity connects to children's experiences with the natural world.

For teachers not to capitalize on children's interest in and curiosity about nature and seize it as an opportunity to teach children to do science is an opportunity missed for fostering scientific literacy.

MISSION IMPOSSIBLE?

Teachers prepared for teaching in self-contained elementary classrooms are not scientifically literate. The science educator's challenge of teaching elementary teacher candidates to value and understand science and the teaching of science is daunting.

In a constructivist-based science classroom, teachers should provide multiple sense-making experiences with objects, events, and relationships in the natural world. Guidance in sense-making (inquiry) should come from the teacher, in the role of the *knowledgeable other*.

Science educators are continually challenged to find ways to do three things simultaneously – teach teachers to learn science, teach teachers to do science, and develop in teachers a capacity to value science enough to teach science to their students. Such challenges compel science educators into a continual search for efficient and impactful instructional approaches that model both the learning of science through inquiry, and the teaching of science through inquiry to children.

Teachers must first become science learners in order to teach their students to become science learners. To teach teachers to do science, teachers must be convinced, by means of their experiences, that doing science is a worthwhile endeavor that can lead them to meaningful learning. Framing this mandate in a constructivist perspective – the meaning of teacher candidates' experiences with science must be changed. This job usually falls to the science educator, who must accomplish such a shift in a very short time frame – usually one to two semesters prior to student teaching.

CHANGING THE MEANING OF TEACHER CANDIDATES' EXPERIENCES WITH SCIENCE

Most elementary teacher candidates see their primary job as that of teaching children to read. The preponderance of literacy-based courses in traditional elementary teacher preparation programs does little to dispel this perception. Three of the four sophomore year education courses in the program in which the course described here resides are devoted to the teaching of language arts. This is extended by requiring four more literacy or literature – based courses in the junior year, where there is one science methods course – Inquiry.

The instructional impact odds are already stacked against the content-based teacher educator in the traditional elementary education program. One fourteen week course is all the science educator often gets to get reluctant science learners more fully engaged in the idea that science is do-able, know-able, and teachable.

To teach the process of scientific inquiry to others, it is necessary to understand at a deep level (largely through making sense of experiences with the process) the successive steps of the inquiry process. Teacher Candidates, for the most part, have not been afforded the opportunity to learn this process during their formal science schooling.

Elementary teacher candidates' attitudes toward science are predominantly negative; and traditional elementary teacher preparation programs, heavily laden with literacy and literature courses, reinforce candidates' perceptions of themselves as reading teachers, not science teachers. Unless something happens to change this perception during their program of teacher training, elementary age children suffer the consequence.

The doing of science is not well taught in the formal school setting, or the preservice elementary teacher would arrive at their first science methods course better aware of and comfortable with science.

Preservice elementary teachers have usually not had the opportunity to construct scientific knowledge in their high school and college laboratory courses. "Experiments" in traditional high school and college science courses are not connected to meaningful descriptive data from the natural world.

Data for experiments is pre-packaged for the learner, not gathered by the learner. The use of seemingly complicated mathematical formulas to manipulate data confounds the idea that anyone can do science, or that science actually begins with records gathered from careful "looking" at natural structures, relationships, or events. In the name of efficient delivery of the maximum amount of content, the learner's thrill of discovery in the natural world is short-circuited.

Being taught science through a truncated version of the traditional "scientific method" with minimal exposure to the natural world or the experiential opportunity to choose and gather one's own "data," leads learners to become disconnected from the aesthetics of the empirical nature of the discipline and disconnects them from the knowledge-making process that gives meaning to the content.

The science educator usually has a single semester in which to change candidates' meaning of their experiences with science. The science educator is continually seeking for methods that accomplish this time-constrained goal. The instructional approach described below was developed over time in a junior level methods course. Use of the Guided Nature Journal as a learning strategy has been successful in changing candidates' attitudes toward science and improving their scientific literacy.

HOW SHOULD THE DOING OF SCIENCE BE TAUGHT?

The process of doing science is teachable. Inquiry is well understood and well defined by many who study knowledge-making (Gowin, 1981).

For purposes of teaching the inquiry process to novice learners, the author created a continuum that engages learners in answering a successively more inclusive set of questions about a particular set of "data," which is defined as anything that is closely observed. These four questions require learners to engage in the stepwise thinking of inquiry, but in a manner accessible to the novice.

- The questions begin with *What?*. *What* questions are answered by the learner generating rich descriptive records of the object, event, or relationship that is being observed.

- The next question is *How?*. To answer the *How*, learners are required to transform their recorded data in ways that allow them to see patterns of relationships.

- Once patterns are found, the next question posed is *Why?*. To answer the *Why* learners must interpret the analyzed data and posit an explanation for the relationships they have uncovered. The explanation could be based in research, or tied to an explanatory framework of a knowledgeable other (the role of the teacher).
- And once an explanation has been posited and defended with the data, learners are asked the *What If?* question. The *What if* requires learners to test the explanatory power and limits of their conclusions reported in the *Why*. The *What if* should lead learners to the next set of inquiry questions, because it demands the gathering of more observations.

Novice learners can be taught to approach any event, setting, or relationship with the purpose of answering these four questions. The first is always *What* and it is the strength of that answer on which the rest of the inquiry lies. So the *What*, which is often described *for* the learner in a traditional science classroom, is a critical step in the inquiry process. Without empowering or expecting the learner to trust their own observations, and think of them as important, ownership of the process of doing science is taken away. The learner comes to view the doing of science as something they cannot do, but that others must do for them. This is the beginning of learned helplessness in science.

The first job of a knowledgeable other (the science educator) is to empower the learner to observe the natural world. The Guided Nature Journal is structured to convey this expectation. The learner is assessed on the depth, detail, and perspective brought to each entry.

WHY NATURE JOURNALING?

Guided nature journaling is a sustainably successful tool for connecting learners to the familiar and then changing the meaning of their experiences with the familiar while engaging them in the process of inquiry. The strategy has been developed by trial and error over time. The impact of the approach can now be seen as teacher candidates have carried this strategy to their own classrooms and report back on their students' enthusiasm for learning through the nature journal.

The Guided Nature Journal is an approach that rests on the idea that a knowledgeable other is available to guide the thinking of the learner and supply criteria by which the learner can judge or advance their thinking, most particularly when answering the *Why* and *What If* questions on the inquiry continuum.

This is done by requiring class participants to closely observe structures, settings, and events in their immediate natural world, and describe them in words, pictures, or drawings. To change the meaning of the learner's experience is a primary constructivist goal. It leads to independent knowledge construction, which is the process of inquiry.

But authentic inquiry has criteria that must be recognized because it is those criteria that measure the value of the knowledge and situate it into a wider context, recognize its power and limits. The role of a knowledgeable other in this process is therefore that of the teacher. But the teacher must experience this process first-hand if they are to teach it to others. And they must also use it as their personal knowledge-making tool to pursue further scientific knowledge as part of their ongoing professional development.

The job of the science educator is two-fold: To create self-directed science learners, and to create teachers who can engage children in the doing and knowing of the natural world and the scientific theories that explain it.

THE GUIDED NATURE JOURNAL AS SUSTAINED INQUIRY

The Inquiry course of which Nature Journaling is a part is structured in the workshop format. Candidates are engaged in sets of highly structured activities, usually in pairs or groups of three or four. The activities focus on building the skills of observing and recording in the nature journal.

Direct instruction in the form of content presentation provides explanatory frameworks from which candidates are expected to transform and synthesize the material in their journal at specified points in the course.

Course activities scaffold the skills of observing and recording. Metacognitive skills of classifying, comparing, organizing, synthesizing, interpreting, and evaluating are modeled and practiced.

Science content is made accessible by the way it is conceptually structured and presented. Candidates are given a three-part conceptual lens through which to frame, analyze, and evaluate their journal records:

1. Observing and recording *structure*
2. Observing and recording *events*
3. Observing and recording *relationships*

SETTING THE STAGE

Prior to the first class meeting candidates are sent a course syllabus that includes detailed notes explaining the purpose and format of the journaling activity. Attached to the notes are sample entries of nature journals created by scientists and naturalists as diverse as Isabella Bird, Lewis and Clark, Isaac Newton, Charles Darwin, and Beatrix Potter.

Candidates are told in the first class meeting that they will be learning the science they need to teach by doing science – not by experimenting, but by recording what they see around them in nature.

Emphasis is put on the accessibility of science to everyone by presenting some drawings and work of Beatrix Potter, something familiar to teacher candidates. The story of Beatrix Potter as a naturalist evolves from looking at her works for children.

The instructor also shares excerpts from nature journals of students of her former candidates to make the case that what they are learning can be carried directly into the classroom.

ESTABLISHING EXPECTATIONS FOR THE QUALITY OF THE JOURNAL

When expectations for content and format of journals are reviewed, the instructor is met with looks of consternation. Questions, such as... "How many entries do we have to do," "What are we supposed to put in the journal," and "I don't really like science/nature," tumble out, one on top of the other. Resistance is being mustered; reluctance and hesitation are palpable.

The commonly expressed attitudes toward nature that emerge are that nature is something to be avoided outside of one's normal routine; or that nature simply serves as an immutable, predictable, two-dimensional backdrop to life, and is therefore uninteresting; Most disturbing of all is the perceived disconnect between science and nature. Early in the course, candidates repeatedly voice the idea that science has nothing to do with nature, since science is mostly experiments.

Added to the dislike of the subject is the reluctance to write. Though most of the candidates in Inquiry have recently completed a required course in expressive writing, they come to this course with little to no experience of descriptive writing.

Because of the unfamiliarity of the journaling task, and their attitudes toward the subject of the journals, course participants will treat the journaling assignment as trite if clear performance expectations are not set and periodically revisited.

During the first class, a Reflection Rubric for the Nature Journal is introduced (Appendix) and discussed at length. Additionally, candidates are shown journal excerpts of work from previous semesters and the rubric scores that each excerpt earned. The instructor includes examples from her own journal as well, and again references some from well-known journalists, past and present.

To insure consistency and ongoing effort, weekly journal checks and conferences with individual journalists are set up and followed throughout the course.

Without exception candidates' reactions are uniform: They view the journaling task as something they have to "get through." Because they have the rubric and examples as a guide, they also know "how much work/effort" they actually have to put into the journal in order to "get a good grade," and thus the semester begins.

BEGINNING WITH STRUCTURES

Introductory journaling tasks must first teach observation and recording, analysis, interpretation, and how to use content criteria to generate, test, and expand explanations of what is observed and recorded. This is the Inquiry continuum. These skills are best learned and taught through the "Structures in Nature" course lens. The skills are then practiced as journalists expand their entries to the Observation of Events (lens 2) and the Analysis of Relationships (lens 3).

Observing and Recording Structures

The classroom where the course is taught is set up as a natural history learning laboratory. There is an extensive collection of objects found in the field by the instructor and by previous course participants. These include bones, shells, feathers, nests, snakes' skins, and dried seaweed from the nearby beaches. It is these objects that candidates must first observe and record.

Candidates are expected to select at least three different objects and devote the first entries in their journals to drawing and describing these objects in great detail. First entries are usually small and lack detail.

The instructor provides a one sheet handout from a drawing book that helps candidates draw what they see, and shows them how to use perspective, shading, and color to realistically portray the object they are observing.

Candidates begin again, and with the aid of jeweler's loops and a hand lens to magnify the detail of the structure, draw the object from multiple perspectives, scaling up important details. Candidates' entries are evaluated by peers and instructors collaboratively, looking for descriptive details, accurate representations, and proportionality of scale in the representation.

Candidates are then required to find three structures in the outdoors and record those structures in their natural setting. They are given the option of using photography or of drawing (the use of both is encouraged).

Candidates are assessed on the depth and breadth of detail they capture. Using the initial feedback from their first two assignments, they are told to continue to make and record observations of structures from the collection and/or from the immediate natural setting. Journals are checked weekly, and progress in capturing detail is noted and discussed.

As candidates build their recording skills, their initial reluctance for the task begins to fade. They bring in contributions for the nature collection and describe them to one another enthusiastically. They start to notice the smaller structures in their environment, and record the symmetry, complexity, and "beauty" of these objects.

Some journalists become focused on a single type of structure. Moss, lichen, mushrooms, leaves, and squirrels have been the focus of some journals over time. Other journalists record a variety of objects. As the journaling progresses, candidates' experiences with the natural world begin to change. The immediate environment that seemed flat and two dimensional, hardly worth noticing, becomes a structure-rich and diverse world.

Objects viewed as previously mundane become, with the observation and recording of detail, interesting, amazing, and personally meaningful. An appreciation for the natural world and an understanding of its complexity develops, and can be seen in the journal entries.

Once journalists have established a repertoire of rich and detailed observations of structure, categories of likenesses and differences emerge naturally from their records. This natural tendency is encouraged, and then expected. Journalists are expected to consult nature guides made available as classroom resources to explore the diversity of structures, and to add facts and detail that contextualizes their observations. For the first time in their lives as "scientists," they seek their own corroborating information from expert sources, and use this information to enrich and extend their entries.

Groupings emerge from analysis of detail. For example, one journalist noticed that the squirrels she had been drawing and photographing were in fact two different species. One was native, and the other "invasive." Another journalist's photographs of leaves in her backyard led to an understanding of likenesses and differences among plants, as well as to an impressive collage of seed structure.

Generating Explanations of Diversity from Observations and Comparisons of Structures

To reinforce journalists' emerging skill at using detailed observations of structure to more finely differentiate one living thing from another, a formal lesson on plant diversity is taught. A simple diagram based on Whittaker's 5 kingdom classification scheme is presented to the class after they have collected, pressed, and prepared leaves collected in the local area.

Candidates use the classification scheme as a reference for identifying their own plants and classifying them according to their structural attributes. Candidates experience the task of organizing data during this activity as they are expected to complete a pre-constructed data sheet. Candidates mount their pressed specimens on herbarium paper, and their collection is added to the nature center's existing herbarium collection. This activity models the way that scientists collect, record, and communicate data on natural structures (Appendix).

A second full class activity extends this idea of diversity as candidates are given the task of finding and recording all types of fungus on the campus grounds. Most specimens are drawn or photographed in situ. Field data is brought back to the nature center where candidates identify the fungi, and extend their work to the creation of a classification scheme that anyone can use quickly to identify mushrooms to type.

EXPANDING THE SKILLS OF INQUIRY TO OBSERVING AND RECORDING EVENTS IN NATURE

Structures are static. Events are moments in time. Capturing an event in a nature journal requires not only the skill of recording detail, but of choosing the detail that will accurately portray the event as it happened. The scale of detail needed to capture an event must be larger than that previously used to capture the detail of structure.

The challenge to the journalist is to put the reader into the setting and accurately portray the event as it happened. This requires more description in words, supported by sketches or photographs, rather than detailed drawings of structures.

Capturing the setting is the next step in understanding and valuing the relationships between living things and their environment. It is these relationships that the major theories of science explain.

CAPTURING EVENTS IN THE NATURE LAB

Candidates begin to capture events by actually capturing specimens to be housed in the nature laboratory. Small groups elect to collect specimens for which habitats have already been established. There is a reptile group, an amphibian group, an invertebrate group, a fish group, a plant group, and sometimes a microorganism group.

The first event usually described in the nature journal is the capture adventure.

Once captured, candidates are expected to engage in research that will allow them to establish a care routine for their collected specimens (which they will release at the end of the semester or the year). They must set up a monitoring and feeding routine, and make time to record the organisms' behavior in their journals. Feeding events, response to stimuli events, and physiological events are recorded as they occur.

Journalists discover and describe behavioral and physiological events as they unfold in the various habitats they observe and monitor. Examples of conclusions drawn from descriptions of events in the nature journal are listed below:

- Crabs do not see food, they "smell" it.
- Crabs move from side to side, not backward and forward.
- Snakes are picky eaters and have different personalities.
- Snakes capture food in water.
- There is more than one kind of "frog."
- Not all amphibians live in the water, but all are born there.
- Turtles bury themselves in the soil and are very territorial.
- If butterflies and moths hatch too soon, they will not be fully developed and die.
- Tadpoles morph into teeny tiny little frogs about a quarter of a centimeter in height and length, and perish before we figure out what to feed them.
- Fish respond by sight to food.
- Some fish stay together and others swim alone.
- Crayfish can live in water and on "land" and are escape artists.
- Snakes can climb up glass and get through very small holes.
- Snakes can jump the length of their body, or more, really fast!
- Plants all look exactly alike when they first emerge from their seeds.
- Snakes, crabs, and crayfish all grow by shedding their "skin" and hiding until their new skin hardens.
- Lots of insects spend time as larvae in the water.
- Mushrooms pop up and disappear fast because the "real" fungus lives under the ground. Those are just the reproductive structures we see.

- A praying mantis bite hurts.
- There is a right way and a wrong way to pick up a snake.
- All animals produce waste and it must be removed on a regular basis when they are confined.

"Cause and Effect"

One reason for bringing nature to the classroom is to be able to observe behavioral and physiological events more closely over longer periods of time. Another reason is for candidates to engage in the "cause and effect" work of science through first-hand experience observing events that give us clues about the interaction between the organism and its environment.

Journalists are expected to experiment with and record the outcomes of their organism's habitat preferences. They are expected to experiment with different foods to see if there are preferences. They are expected to record all outcomes of these events, and draw inferences about their organisms' habitats. This should be corroborated by research and more trial and error to maximize a match to the organism's natural environment.

Capturing Events in Nature

Journalists are expected to "travel" with their journal throughout the time of the course. As a result they capture and relate many events in a variety of natural settings.

Personal voice is seen in their descriptions of these settings. When capturing an event in the setting, candidates are able to tap into their previous expressive writing experience, and it is in these entries where the journalist's evolving reactions to and appreciation of natural events can be tracked.

Generating an Understanding of Niche, Habitat, Adaptation from Descriptions of Events

Once journalists have built a repertoire of events, a content presentation lesson provides explanation of a concept map that candidates will use to define the concepts of niche, habitat and adaptation. Candidates are expected to do in-depth research on one particular organism or group of organisms in a particular local ecological community and create a concept map of their own that illustrates their ability to tie examples of adaptations to the concepts of habitat and niche.

Journalists are asked to examine their own entries and group some of their observations by type of adaptation, or similar habitat. This task helps them relate their experiences with essential scientific concepts, and extends their understanding of the concepts that go beyond a simple memorized definition, tying personal experiences to the meaning of the concept.

Analyzing Relationships in the Natural World by Evaluating Journal Entries

Throughout the journal, while candidates described structures and events, they were also describing specific relationships. When they compared and contrasted organisms by their structures or described the interactions of organisms with their environments, or simply described an event, they were unavoidably describing relationships in nature.

The final meta-cognitive skill that is taught is requiring journalists to revisit their entries and look for these relationships and organize them around a theme, such as "system" or "change," or a subordinate theme that speaks to relationships between living things and their environments and among living things themselves.

Relationships in nature are modeled and practiced in two structured whole class activities. The first is a half day field trip to a local ecological community. Candidates are expected to observe, record, and collect evidence of organisms in the setting. Candidates organize their observational data, and are expected to construct a food web of the community from their data. They are also expected to identify the ecological niche (functionally and spatially) for each organism in their database.

The second activity is a content presentation lesson on the cell theory and levels of organization of living things. Using this explanatory framework, candidates are expected to re-visit their journals and create a relational hierarchy of the organisms they observed.

Drawing Theoretical Themes from Analysis of Journal Entries

The journalist's culminating activity requires them to organize their journal data under a major scientific theory or theme (as presented in the NRC, AAAS, and state science standards); and to communicate the theme, using examples from their journals, in a power point presentation to the class.

Titles have included: "Art in Nature" (theme: Elements and principles of design in nature), "Eating to Survive" (theme: Natural Selection), and "Simple to Complex" (theme: Cell Theory).

Alternatively, candidates are encouraged to find their own themes, but they must be embedded in the national science standards. Many themes, such as "Art in Nature," and another titled "Poetry in Nature" showed how well candidates could incorporate ideas from other disciplines into the presentation of rich and valid science content.

IMPACT OF THE GUIDED NATURE JOURNALING EXPERIENCE

Through analysis of journals, course products, and anecdotal records several assertions can be made about the impact of journaling on candidates' attitudes toward science and their scientific literacy.

- Assertion 1: Candidates' perceptions of nature change. Nature is interesting, has depth, and detail worth noticing (and getting excited about).
- Assertion 2: Candidates' understanding of science changes from that of "something scientists do in a lab" to "a human endeavor accessible to all."
- Assertion 3: Candidates can connect their experiences in the natural world to scientific theories.
- Assertion 4: Candidates carry the journaling to their classrooms and incorporate it into their teaching of science.

The effectiveness of the approach is best witnessed when candidates have completed the program and become teachers. They often return with pictures, drawings, or stories about what they continue to witness in the natural world. Others send examples of their students' work in their nature journals. Such evidence lends support to the transferability of the journal as an effective method to build and pass on scientific literacy from teacher to student.

CONCLUSIONS

The Guided Nature Journal has proven a successful change strategy for making science accessible and understandable to preservice elementary and middle school teachers.

Participants, with guidance in reflection on the records in their journal, discover what they have learned can be used as examples that give personal meaning to previously abstractly presented scientific concepts, principles, and theories.

Applying analytical, interpretive, explanatory, and evaluative thinking to records, guides participants' development of their journal into an authentic scientific investigation of the natural world. As the journal progresses, course participants are periodically required to analyze and synthesize their journal records into a "theme" which is publicly defended and evaluated for scientific authenticity. Thus the journalists are guided to experience the complete process of inquiry – from record-keeping to communicating meaning to others.

Guided Nature Journaling has proven to engage teachers in the *doing* of science in a non-threatening way that they perceive as accessible to themselves as learners. The Guided Nature Journaling experience has been shown to change teachers' perceptions of the value of teaching science and to provide them with a replicable model for teaching science to their future students.

The inquiry course is conducted as design-based research. Instructional approaches are changed or altered in response to analysis of successive iterations of candidate products and class artifacts. Evidence continues to support the assertions built from analysis of artifacts, and supports the value claim that Guided Nature Journaling as sustained activity is an impactful tool for creating change and change agents for the fostering of scientific literacy.

REFERENCE

Gowin, D. B. (1981). *Educating*. Ithaca, NY: Cornell University Press.

APPENDIX

Knowledge Construction through the Process of Scientific Inquiry
  Scoring Scale:

  1= no evidence for indicator, unacceptable;
  2=some evidence for indicator, passing but needs improvement;
  3= acceptable evidence for indicator, meets minimum course requirements but not professionally ready;
  4= regular evidence for indicator, professionally ready, novice teacher candidate;
  5= exceptional evidence for indicator, professionally ready meritorious teacher candidate

Benchmarks and their indicators that should guide entries in The Nature Journal:
  Benchmark I: Descriptive Knowledge
  First-hand observations of objects, events and/or settings are accurately recorded to capture their richness, detail, and complexity using multiple representations.
  Indicators:

  1. Pictorial representations are detailed, accurate, labeled. 1 2 3 4 5

2. Pictorial representations have multiple perspectives that allow for completeness of not - ordinarily- observed details making them easily seen with ordinary vision. 1 2 3 4 5
3. Written observations supplement the detail of pictorial representations. 1 2 3 4 5
4. Written and pictorial observations describe critical attributes of an object, event, or setting, indicating careful and deep observation. 1 2 3 4 5

Score:

Benchmark II. Transformational Knowledge

Descriptive (observational) data was analyzed in depth, recorded in the journal and enabled the author to create scientifically accurate categories of likenesses and differences that then enabled them to generate scientifically authentic interpretations, also recorded in the journal.

Indicators: The journal author...

1. Categorized, compared, and grouped first-hand observations based on essential characteristics of the object, event, or setting and displayed these graphically or in tables in the journal. 1 2 3 4 5
2. Provided written summaries of patterns of likenesses and differences based on categorical data. 1 2 3 4 5
3. Used generalized descriptive observations as a basis to postulate scientific arguments or explanations; and to formulate questions that can be answered by further first–hand investigation, and/or scientific research. 1 2 3 4 5
4. Cited multiple primary resources. 1 2 3 4 5

Score:

Benchmark III. Explanatory Knowledge

Through research and scientific inquiry based in first-hand observations of objects, events or settings, the journal author has postulated a personally constructed explanation of a scientific concept, principle, or theory using scientific argumentation.

Indicators: The journal author ...

1. Created and communicated a major scientific theme based in authentic knowledge of scientific theory, principle or concept. 1 2 3 4 5
2. Clearly grounded and supported scientific explanations in recorded and interpreted data in the journal. 1 2 3 4 5

Score:

Benchmark IV. Evaluation

Journal author can evaluate their own knowledge-construction process using the criteria of scientific inquiry and can formulate scientific explanations grounded in scientific argumentation that demonstrate knowledge growth in the essential concepts, principles and theories of science.

Indicators: The journal author...

1. Summatively sorted the type of knowledge in entries as descriptive, transformative, or explanatory. 1 2 3 4 5
2. Formatively and summatively evaluated the quality of each type of knowledge citing specific examples from the journal. 1 2 3 4 5
3. Formatively set and implemented written goals that substantively improved the scientific quality of subsequent journal entries. 1 2 3 4 5
4. Summatively evaluated their depth and breadth of scientific knowledge using criteria from the national science standards and scientific texts. 1 2 3 4 5

Score:

Turning Point: Leaf Collecting

Ivey Mask, Graduate Student, Journal Entry

I love nature. It's surprising. It's beautiful and dynamic. Most of all it can reduce my stress. So why would I want to do a college-required nature journaling activity while on a walk through the park when I'm trying to relax from the pressures of life? The two are diametrically opposed.

So, there I was, Dr. P., trying to get some exercise on a walk/run through Silver Lake Park. I was *not* thinking about how everything around me could relate to my nature journal for your class.

However, I spotted a grove of River Birch Trees that I love to walk through, and yes observe, but casually mind you. I was certain they were River Birch because I had planted several of the same kind in my yard. Anyway, as I neared the grove of birches I remembered a photo I took of a ladybug on what I thought was a River Birch leaf. The ladybug photo sparked my curiosity so I paused to observe the leaves on one of the River Birches in the grove. Then I noticed that the leaves on the tree next to it looked identical, yet it was obviously a different kind of tree, there was entirely different looking bark.

So, I took a leaf from each tree, held them next to each other, and was comparing details when it hit me! *I was not doing this for my nature journal.*

I know this makes you happy, Dr. P. I am now pressing the leaves and plan to peruse the similarities and differences when they dry.

Chapter Six

Story in the Classroom

Jamie Whitman-Smithe

"To live is to change, to acquire the words of a story, and that is the only celebration we mortals really know" (Kingsolver, 2005, p. 385).

An appreciation for the art of storytelling usually begins at a young age when parents share stories about their own lives. For example, a mother might tell stories about being raised on a peach ranch in Colorado, or a father might tell stories about being raised in a large family in Minnesota. Consequently, adults who have grown up in the tradition of storytelling may choose to continue this tradition within the framework of their own families.

This same group of adults may also choose to integrate story into their chosen careers. For example, comedians use story to entertain audience members, physicians use story to relax their patients, and teachers use story to set the stage for the next lesson. Sometimes, teachers, who fall into the abovementioned category of appreciating the art of storytelling, are reluctant to integrate story into their own classrooms for various reasons. If this teacher-description sounds familiar - read on.

THE TEACHING LIFE

When new teachers begin to live the teaching life, they soon realize that they have two major expectations placed upon them: first, teachers are expected to continue to develop personally and professionally, and second, teachers are expected to provide students with a safe learning environment as well as to continuously develop and teach effective classroom lessons. A vehicle that some teachers may use to enhance their personal/professional development as well as to teach effective lessons is *story*.

Story is an economical way to express oneself to others. When one takes the time to think about the cost of story, one realizes that the actual cost of story is *time*. That is the time it takes to imagine (or retrieve) the story. In other words, story is available 24/7. Story is the retrieval of memory nuggets that allow the individual to tell how life *is*, how life *was*, or how life can be *imagined*. Story is many things - but, story is not - technology. In other words, story is a bargain and available to all.

TYPES AND KINDS OF STORY

There are many types of story. The following are some examples:

- Stories we tell about our experiences (In the late 1980s I traveled to India...)
- Stories that we imagine (I lay in bed on Christmas Eve and I could hear...)
- Stories that are told to us about others' experiences (In the late 1940s Aunt Rose sacrificed her four year college scholarship to stay home and...)
- Stories that teachers mine from students (Tell us how your families prepare for ...)
- Stories that teachers mine from the literature (Infants who are developing ...)

Teachers who have chosen to employ story (whereby they reflect on past experiences in order to extend their self-knowledge or become aware of personal issues that need attention) are honing their instrument (*themselves* so they will be able to present their best selves to their students day after day in the classroom and also be clear of mind when planning curricula and preparing and teaching lessons - similar to actors who use various methods to hone themselves so they can bring their best selves to the preparation of a new role) for living the teaching life.

Some examples of the uses of story in the classroom are as follows:

- To assess what students have learned (students write reports describing what happened during field experiences),
- To weave pieces of material together from the literature or notes in such a way as to create an interesting story to present to students,
- To organize descriptive data that students have brought to class,
- To draw students' attention to important information,
- To outline pieces of information included in a historical backdrop,
- To summarize experiences that students have shared and how the experiences connect to theory.

The use of story in the classroom helps the teacher continue to promote a safe, stress-free environment for all students, an environment in which children feel that they are treated with respect and in which it is okay to make mistakes. Most teachers understand that when children feel safe and respected, they will relax and learn

STORY AND CELEBRITY

One celebrity teacher is the late Frank McCourt, a practicing Irish Catholic and constructivist, who was born in the United States, and raised in Ireland from the age of four. McCourt recounted his life in three volumes beginning with his childhood (*Angela's Ashes*), followed by his move to the United States at the age of eighteen (*'Tis*), and ending with a book filled with stories about his teaching life in a New York City public high school (*Teacher Man*).

McCourt's storytelling brought to him a late-in-life celebrity as well as numerous awards, honors, and travel opportunities. The point being, as a rule, most people enjoy a story. The following pages will include specific examples of how *story* has been used in a constructivist classroom to promote a clear understanding of what is being taught.

EXAMPLES OF STORY USED BY A CONSTRUCTIVIST PROFESSOR

Child Development

In a child development class teachers may choose to lay a foundation of child development information by beginning with the three principles of development that are agreed upon by most developmental psychologists (Woolfolk, 2001).

- Everyone learns at their own rate, (for example, children learn to smile, talk at different ages)
- Development is relatively orderly, (for example, children crawl, then walk, then run)
- Development happens over time, (for example, children begin to read by first looking at picture books, move on to chapter books, and later, Harry Potter).

A traditional teacher might choose to communicate the three principles of development to students by writing the principles on the board and telling the students what they mean, or by asking the students if they can give an example of each principle. However, a constructivist teacher might begin the preparation of this lesson by asking herself the question, "How can the environment in a constructivist classroom be set so students can do the following...

- Determine the three principles of development from the evidence that has been offered,
- Internalize the three principles of development,
- Eventually, retrieve the three principles to be used for future problem-solving episodes?"

In other words, one of the goals of a constructivist teacher is to provide assistance when the task can *only* be completed with assistance.

So the constructivist teacher, in order to meet the goal of identifying the three principles of development, requires the students to call or go home and ask their parents for the following pieces of information:

- type of birth (vaginal or C-section),
- C-section, planned or unplanned,
- weight,
- length,
- breast fed or bottle fed,
- first smiled,
- cut first tooth,
- age first crawled,
- age spoke first word,
- age potty trained,
- age began to read.

Upon returning to class, students write their personal data on the board. Opportunities for students to tell stories begin with this question, "What did your parents say when you asked for this information?" In that way stories begin to evolve from the data written on the board.

For example, some of the C-sections were planned, and some were unplanned. Some of the births were premature. Premature births usually come with stories about difficulty meeting milestones of development. Other stories evolve with respect to learning how to read, toilet training, and first words; especially when the first word is "No."

After the students' personal data have been sufficiently noted and discussed through storytelling, students are then asked to look at the data written below each section heading on the board such as Type of Birth, Length, etc., and then look at the data written across the board. From these data, students are asked to deduce the three principles of development (*everyone develops at their own rate, development is relatively orderly, development takes place over time*). If students cannot immediately identify the principles then it is the teacher's turn to tell a story in order to open up student-thinking.

For the principle that states that *there is an order to development*, the teacher tells this story: mom and dad bring their two-day-old son, little Sammy, home from the hospital and place him very carefully in his new crib. Mom and dad look at their first-born lovingly before going down to the kitchen to eat lunch.

After a few minutes, mom and dad sit down to eat lunch, but before they begin to eat they call up the stairs to Little Sammy to tell him that it is time for lunch. Shortly thereafter, the infant son, Little Sammy, climbs out of the crib and comes down the stairs, walks to the kitchen, sits in a chair at the table, places a napkin under his chin, takes a fork and digs in. Little Sammy tells mom and dad that he is really hungry because it was a lot of work wiggling his way down through his mom's birth canal a couple of days ago. Mom and dad look at little Sammy and smile in agreement. Mom tells Little Sammy that there is plenty of food for seconds.

After this story is told, the teacher asks the students if, as a newborn, any of them had exhibited any of these behaviors with their parents on their first day home from the hospital. When the answer of, "No" is given, the discussion opens up and students begin to break down the examples given in the story in order to explain why an infant would never exhibit these behaviors. Eventually, students begin to understand and are able to articulate clearly the principle *there is an order to development*.

After the three principles of development have been identified, the next discussion that comes up is, "Why is this information important?" and "How will homes and/or classrooms be affected if parents and/or teachers are not aware of the three principles of development?"

It is clear from the aforementioned example that rather than telling the students the principles of development and asking for examples, the students in this constructivist classroom leave with new pieces of information that have been attached to their own personal stories. This transfer of information resulted from an assignment that required students to collect personal data that students' parents were able to supply by means of outstanding memories and/or well-kept baby books (*story*).

It is important to note that the students in this constructivist classroom own all of the information that was shared during the lesson, whereby they explored the three principles of development. This example illustrates how a constructivist teacher plans and orchestrates a lesson that includes knowledge construction exercises that promote learning that is deeper than rote learning/memorization.

TEACHING A DEVELOPMENTAL THEORY

In order to set up the classroom environment to begin teaching a particular child developmental theory, the constructivist teacher considers the following question: "How can the environment in a constructivist classroom be set up so students can project their personal experience into the tenants of the theory that is being presented in the day's lesson?"

The traditional teacher might begin by providing students with a historical backdrop of the theory, a report on the beliefs of the theorist, and an explanation of the theory; presented through PowerPoint slides, overheads, while students listen and write notes. In fact this was the original method used by in the early years of teaching a course on child development theory. Fortunately, boredom and reflection drove the novice to begin the process of transforming the course steeped in traditional methodology to a course that exudes the constructivist philosophy.

Not sure where to begin, the teacher finally proceeded by rewriting the class notes with bright colored pens each semester (secretly harboring the belief that repetition of note-writing would produce change). Eventually, the teacher began to notice that each time the notes were re-written they were different. The notes began to feel more familiar, less stilted. The teacher persevered and each semester new ideas gradually opened up and these ideas would eventually lead to *story*.

For example, the teacher decided that instead of using the term "baby" when talking about the actual theory, the students would benefit if the teacher were to say, "When we were born, when we were babies, when our parents brought us home..." Why? Because a course on child development is actually a course about all of us as fellow humans.

Gradually, instead of presenting a set of cold notes to students, a story began to take shape. Gradually, the teacher began to feel like a story-teller rather than a theory-presenter. During the course-sculpting process, the teacher imagined mastery over the traditional methodology once practiced.

Eventually a story was mined from each of the three theories taught in the child development course; theories by Piaget, Vygotsky, and Erikson. For example, Piaget (1995) constructed a theory that delineates four stages of cognitive development.

Story in the Classroom 103

With respect to Piaget's first stage of cognitive development, the Sensorimotor Stage that covers birth to two-years of age, the teacher decided that it was important for students to examine the question, "How do your families prepare for the birth of a new baby?"

Students were placed in groups and asked to discuss the customs that are practiced in their families. Students reported many interesting customs, such as families that have members who take turns planning family baby showers. Some baby showers are attended by men and women, who in turn give large gifts. Additionally, in some families, after the baby is born family and friends visit the new parents and bring more gifts. Other families hang banners, play party games, and eat and drink as if they were attending a wedding.

Next, it is at this point in the class that the teacher takes over to summarize the information that has been discussed thus far and to change the direction of the class from familial customs to the introduction of Piaget and his four stages of cognitive development. Students are led to see that after all of the parties, gifts, and well wishes, eventually most expectant parents go to the hospital to await the birth of their baby.

Now that students have discussed their own families' baby-welcoming customs, they are ready to learn about Piaget's four stages of cognitive development. At this point the teacher continues with story: "When *we* were born we were all wet and slippery—bereft of all baggage—and *we* immediately began to construct basic schemes such as sucking and squirming with only our senses and our motor development (or our ability to move). [Note: schemes, according to Piaget, are structures used to organize incoming information.]

At this intersection, Piaget is introduced as the character in the story whose theory was constructed to inform parents of the milestones their children will be meeting throughout childhood. Students are told that the most developmental growth in a human's life takes place between birth and two years of age, and that while much of the development that takes place produced excitement for us as babies as well as for our parents, at the same time it is important to note that developmental growth also involves change in the construction of schemes (organizing incoming information) and thus produces *stress*.

For example, a child decides to find out what treasures are located in mom's dresser drawer. This requires the child to decide to find the treasures, to pull a chair over to the dresser, to climb the chair, and to pull open the dresser drawer. This treasure-finding behavior requires the child to combine different behaviors in order to reach the goal. Cognitively, the child is organizing and reorganizing schemes. Initiating these new behaviors can produce a feeling of mastery over the child's environment. At the same time engaging in these new behaviors can overly tire the child; producing stress and a cranky baby.

Thus the aforementioned story that has been mined from Piaget's first stage of cognitive development that focuses on the fact that throughout this sensorimotor stage of cognitive development, infants' and toddlers' cognitive development experiences can be stress-producing. Often when a child in this age range (0-2) is cranky, parents deduce that the child is wet, hungry, or teething, but crankiness can be caused by growth in cognitive development.

This story humanizes the first stage of cognitive development and highlights the fact that at birth babies are born with the use of their senses and motor development (movement), and it is through the use of these abilities over the course of the next two years that babies learn to crawl, walk, talk, and feed themselves as well as develop language.

The challenge then, of teachers who want their students to experience a more in depth learning of the information presented in class, is to mine the story within each subject that is being taught. For example, a course about exceptional children can be introduced as, "This is the Story of the Laws of Special Education," or "This is the Story of Children with Disabilities and What Has to Happen So They Can Receive Services." These titles are examples of the beginning of the story, and from this point the story may begin to unfold over time.

THE DIVERSE SCHOOL

In another course called Diverse School, students explore the concept of diversity and at the same time go out into the community to observe classrooms, attend school board meetings, and interview teachers. On the first day in a traditional classroom, the teacher would typically define and give examples of research about diversity taken from the course-assigned text book. Textbook chapters would be listed in the syllabus and assigned to be read and discussed in class to prepare for later tests for which information would be memorized and promptly forgotten.

On the first day in a constructivist classroom the teacher might begin the course with the introduction of four trade books that tell the story of diversity in four persons' lives; persons of varying ages and backgrounds. Assigning four trade books ensures that students learn about diversity from various individuals rather than one author's opinion found in a single textbook.

For this course of study, the story of diversity was mined in the following ways: The first class assignment requires students to bring specific examples (story) of diversity from their *personal* lives to class where they sit in groups and share their personal stories. Next the main topics of discussion are written on the board. As a class, all look at the topics on the board and class members choose the first topic they care to discuss. Class members participate in the discussion that follows until all topics are addressed.

The next assignment requires students to bring in examples of diversity in their *academic* lives for discussion. This way story is used to help students identify how diversity has affected their lives both personally and academically.

Besides the aforementioned classroom exercises, students go out into the community to observe examples of diversity by completing the following assignments:

- Observe a middle school classroom,
- Attend a local school board meeting,
- Interview an educational professional who has taught at least ten years in the community.

Students are asked to write thick descriptions of what took place, followed by an analysis. Back in the classroom, students share their experiences through group discussions and story. Finally, students write their own story in their philosophy of education essay assignment where, among other topics, they discuss all of the persons who have offered them emotional support when they were growing up, and subsequently, how these experiences have affected their lives.

To prepare for the last day of class, students review and record important points from the diversity exercises and all returned assignments. Back in class, after dividing into groups, students compare notes, discuss them, and set out to piece together a definition of diversity that works for their group.

After definitions are written on the board, they are introduced this way, "On this day (say day and date) at this time (look at the clock and read the time) group # (number of group) tells us that diversity is…(read definition)." Students are reminded that they are the authors of this definition. All students then write down all definitions, the names of the authors (themselves), the date, and the time. Thus the students are provided with a final record of their semester-long work.

According to constructivism, individuals who have participated in knowledge construction experiences will be able to more easily make connections to other courses and retrieve the information for problem-solving situations. Obviously, that is what has happened to the students in the Diverse School class. On the last day of class, students pulled all of the information from the assigned experiences and constructed definitions of diversity that were unique to each of the classroom groups.

Some might say why not ask students to write a definition at the beginning of the semester and then another one at the end? The answer is that the plan of this constructivist teacher is to allow the students the freedom to explore/experience diversity without the expectation of change.

Is it important that the student definitions match the definitions from dictionaries? The answer is that it is important that the students in the Diverse School course experienced (without pressure) all of the knowledge construction activities that the class offered, and then from these experiences constructed/articulated what they believe to be their best definition of diversity.

CLASS JOURNALS

Another form of story is called the Class Journal. This technique is used to inform students' storytelling abilities in such a way that they will have a record of what took place in class, and also so students will be able to think creatively by entering the world of *make believe*.

The Class Journal format requires students to take on the role of a journalist and write thick descriptions of what took place in class that day along with *how* and *why* it happened.

The last section in the Class Journal format asks students to enter the world of *what if?* Students are asked to erase all time, money, and reality constraints (death is an example - even dead people can become class guests) and envision the class being taught in an *ideal* situation including materials, place, and guests. Students are reminded that the *What If* section is not meant as a critique of the class but to provide an opportunity to think creatively. In other words, students are asked to tell a story of what they believe to be the ideal class every day at the end of the class they have just experienced.

THE EXCEPTIONAL CHILD

In this constructivist course about exceptional children or children with disabilities, books that tell the stories of children with disabilities are assigned. Six books are read: four are true stories and the other two are based on real life stories. Also included in classroom presentations are DVDs that tell true stories of disabled persons' lives (see the Appendix for book and DVD titles).

Guests, usually parents, are invited to tell the story of what it was like when they heard for the first time that their child had a disability; sometimes parents and children come together to tell their stories to the class. Guests provide students with opportunities to ask questions. Oftentimes class members have siblings with disabilities, and they want to find out from the guests how having a child with a disability has affected the relationships with their spouses and their other children.

Also in this course, students spend time with a *buddy*, a student of their same age who has either a cognitive disability or autism. During this 10-week-10-hour relationship, students and their buddies, choose a goal to work on together. At the end of the semester students write the story of meeting their buddies, working on the goals, and the results. These stories are often very long, in the twenty-page range.

Students then present to their fellow classmates a brief version of their experience in a Power Point presentation. Students are proud of the accomplishments they have made in another person's life as well as the social/emotional, cognitive, and sometimes motor development growth they have also experienced.

Various assignments offered in this course provide students with vehicles to learn to read scholarly journal articles, to view the work of scholars critically, to collect data that are used to write a research paper, to use the American Psychological Association (APA) format to apply to the paper and References section, and to add to their already broad understanding of diversity and development that they began working on the year before. At the end of the course, it is clear that all of these scholarly skills have been nurtured by the use of story in the classroom (rather than lecturing facts and statistics): student story, story in books, story in video, and story from guests.

POP-UP STORIES

It is important that teachers respect and trust themselves enough to be willing to share a story that "pops up" during the teaching of a lesson. When a story pops up, it is important that the story be shared with the class. It is important because it may be *a* story that at least one of the student's needs to hear on that day at that time.

The story can be prefaced by, "I just thought of something..." or "That reminds me of something...." If for some reason it is not possible to share the story at that moment (no time left in the class period) a good idea is to jot down a few words as a reminder on the lesson plan, so the story can be shared during the next class.

Chapter 6

STUDENT FIT

Finally, in order for any subject matter to be taught successfully, it is important that students understand where they fit into the subject matter; that is, students must be able to finish the following statements, "I need to know the information taught in this course because..." Or, "The information I am being taught in this course will help me in the future because..." Thus the story of the *students' continual assurance that they fit into the content of the course* must be woven into the daily narrative of class work. This story, along with whatever modes of story students bring to share, will result in numerous knowledge construction experiences that translate into learning experiences.

For example, the teacher scrawls Vygotsky's (1978) theory of cognitive development across the board and reads it to the class and says, "Vygotsky tells us that when children interact with caring adults or more advanced peers in a cultural setting, using cultural tools, the child internalizes the meaning of the interaction twice—the first time during the interaction and the second time when the interaction has been completed. Then Vygotsky tells us that as a result of this interaction, the child advances his cognitive development."

Next, the teacher shares an example from her own life. The teacher tells the class when she was nine-years-old and in the fourth grade her Aunt Rose was visiting and agreed to teach her how to knit. The interaction was knitting, the cultural setting was the living room, the cultural tools were the yarn, knitting needles, and the pattern. During the actual knitting lessons, she remembers internalizing that it was hard to sit and concentrate and that it was easy to make mistakes.

When the lessons were completed she remembers feeling proud of herself because she could sit still and knit, and if she made a mistake she could tear the stiches out and begin again. The teacher also remembers how much fun it was to knit items like baby booties and stocking caps to give as gifts.

After the class has thoroughly explored all parts of Vygotsky's theory, the teacher brings the lesson to a close by asking the students for examples of experiences they have shared with their class members. One student answers, "writing theories in a group." Another, "writing papers about their day care visits." The teacher answers, "Yes," but she is looking for an answer that would fit with Vygotsky's theory. Finally, a student answers that as a class each member has visited children at the day care.

For one last time the teacher walks along the board and fills in the sections of Vygotsky's theory that will include the students' shared experience. The teacher asks the students to identify the *caring adults*. A student answers, "the teachers at the day care" and then realizes that in this situation *he* is one of the caring adults.

Then the teacher asks the students what the *interactions* were that the students engaged in with the children. The students answer with reading, playing, and talking with the children, as well as administering various developmental assessment tasks such as classification and conservation. The teacher asks the students what the *cultural setting* was and the students answer the day care. The teacher asks the students what the *cultural tools* were and the students answer blocks, books, and various toys.

The teacher tells the students that she realizes that they are not the children from the day care but that she is going to ask them (students) to place themselves in the children's shoes and think for a minute about what the children might have *internalized* as a result of their six one-hour visits and their participation in the developmental assessment tasks. The students think for a moment and finally answer that the children might feel like "we are their friends," "they trust us," and "they are more confident."

Finally, the teacher tells the students, "When you were given the assignment to go to the day care to work with children you carried out the assignment because it was required and because you wanted the grade." The students agree. "But according to Vygotsky, the interactions that you have had with the children have allowed the children to advance their cognitive development. According to Vygotsky each and every time you interacted with the children their cognitive development was advanced.

Now, the teacher continues, think ahead a few years when you have graduated from college, you have been hired as a teacher, and you have your own classroom. Think of all of the times during the day that you are interacting with your students, and then realize as a result of your interactions with your students—your students will have advanced their cognitive development.

And think again, a few years later, when some of the excitement in becoming a teacher has worn off. It's a rainy Monday morning and you do not want to get out of bed. You want to roll over and go back to sleep. Think for a moment about all of the opportunities you will have missed to interact with your students and advance their cognitive development. Don't waste a moment. It's time to jump out of bed and begin another day in your teaching life!

REFERENCES

Kingsolver, B. (2005). *The poisionwood Bible*. New York: First Harper Perennial Modern Classics.
Piaget, J. (1995). *The essential Piaget*. Northvale, NJ: Jason Aronson Inc.
Woolfolk, A. (2001). *Educational psychology*. (8th edition). Boston: Allyn & Bacon.
Vygotsky, L. (1978). *Mind in society: The development of higher psychological processes.* Cambridge, MA: Harvard University Press.

APPENDIX

Trade Books used for Exceptional Child Course:
    Axline, V. (1964). *Dibs: In search of self.* New York: Ballantine.
    Garfield, J. B. (1994). *Follow my leader.* New York: Puffin.
    Grandin, T., & Scariano, M. M. (1986) *Emergence: Labeled autistic.* New York: Warner.
    Helfman, E. (1993). *On being Sarah.* Morton Grove, IL: Albert Whitman & Co.
    Kingsley, J., & Levitz L. (1994). *Count us in: Growing up with Down syndrome.* New York: Harcourt Brace.
    Pitts, B. (2009). *Step out on nothing: How faith and family helped me conquer life's challenges.* New York: St. Martin's Press.

DVDs used for Exceptional Child Course:
    Freedom machines (2005). New Day Films.
    Hope through heart songs (2006). C-Span.
    Sound and fury (2001). Docu Rama.
    Through your eyes (2007). Hands Free Entertainment.

Turning Point: Teaching Molly

Megan Stoffa, Teacher Candidate

Although I had declared Education as my major, privately I was unsure about what I really wanted to do with my life. My trepidation of the future increased when I learned that I would be working with a class of autistic and mentally challenged students in a course called Exceptional Child. I had never worked with students with disabilities. Could I do this?

I was assigned to be buddies with Molly, a nineteen year old who needed to learn how to fix breakfast meals using a microwave oven. As she practiced preparing meals I began to learn more about her. She had dreams for the future – much like me. She could be aggressive and impatient – much like me. She had problems and roadblocks in life – yes, much like me. Our sessions together opened my eyes to disabilities, to teaching, to people.

Molly and I made great progress that semester. She learned to cook breakfast burritos, bacon, eggs, sausage, pancakes, and waffles. And I learned some teaching techniques that work.

For example, Molly had to *see* the process before she could *do* it. So, the first week I modeled how to do each task and walked her slowly through the steps. The next week we did the same meal, but Molly worked independently and asked me questions when she needed guidance. We celebrated Molly's achievements by reflecting on her cooking experiences while we ate the meal she had prepared.

Finding and learning teaching techniques that worked with Molly became a pleasure for me. Practicing patience and helping Molly make connections from the class to her own life became a habit. Working with her has taught me so much about being a teacher and working with students. She made it easy for me to begin the teaching process.

Molly is eager to learn and has a dream to become a chef later in life. Will she reach her goal of working professionally in a restaurant? I don't know, but she's going to go for it. Working with Molly has ignited my passion to become a special education teacher. Can I do it? Thanks to Molly I think I can.

Chapter Seven

Helping Teacher Candidates Develop the Skills of Reflective Practitioners

Marcia P. Lawton

What is a reflective practitioner? Reflection is something that everyone does all day long; noticing, interpreting, and acting on information in our daily lives. This might be what Schon (1987) calls "reflection-in-action."

Dewey (1933) described reflection as "turning a subject over in the mind and giving it serious and consecutive consideration, thereby enabling us to act in a deliberate and intentional fashion. Reflection involves active, persistent and careful consideration" (p. 9).

These definitions lack specificity of the kind needed to support candidates' development of pedagogy-related reflection strategies and skills. Following a review of research on reflection, Roskos, Vukelich, & Risko (2001) concluded that there was need for "applied research ... to identify and articulate proven strategies for improving students' (candidates') reflective abilities within dynamic teaching-learning environments" (p. 618).

In an attempt to bring more precise meaning to reflection that would support improving reflective abilities for teacher candidates, this author has defined reflection as a recursive process based on methods of action research and including four types of activity:

- Descriptive – refers to information gathering or data collection
- Transformative – the analysis of the information or data collected
- Explanatory – interpreting the analyses, staying close to the data
- Extension – applying the interpretations, critiquing or evaluating, asking questions, developing goals for action.

See Table 7.1 for the Reflection Rubric. Versions of the Reflection Rubric can also be found in Patterson, this volume, although indicators within the four types of activity are somewhat different from course to course depending on the content of the course. The rubric is used throughout the teacher education program.

This is a very recognizable sequence of actions, especially to those who spend time doing research. The classroom teacher needs to be a teacher researcher. Teachers who take a research stance in their classrooms – who consistently think like researchers – will be better able to provide children with *what* is needed *when* it is needed.

The reflective practitioner construct exists in at least three somewhat different forms: reflection as part of a process of constructing content knowledge (reflecting on personal knowledge), reflection on pedagogical practices – usually in the form of analysis of teaching (reflecting on practice), and reflection on the performance of children (assessment of student learning).

This chapter will deal with the third form – the role of reflection in assessment of student learning. (See Patterson, this volume, for reflecting on personal content knowledge.)

BUILDING SKILL IN ASSESSMENT OF STUDENT LEARNING THROUGH REFLECTIVE PRACTICE IN A LITERACY METHODS COURSE

This description focuses on a course taught by the author for many years. The course is called "Assessment and Instruction of Children with Literacy Problems" and was built around a clinical model in which candidates tutor a first or second grader twice a week for about ten weeks. Candidates study and use Marie Clay's (2005) lesson model including:

- Taking daily running records
- Rereading familiar books
- Introducing and helping children read new books
- Guiding writing using Elkonin boxes for phonemic awareness and letter/sound correspondence

The Clay model was chosen because of its focus on the need for a skillful teacher. It provides support (a scaffolded lesson format) for the beginning reading teacher without dictating specific actions which need to be taken by the teacher.

Table 7.1: Reflection Rubric

Scoring key: 1= no evidence, 2=some evidence, 3=acceptable evidence, 4=regular evidence, 5=exemplary evidence

1. *Descriptive Knowledge (Data Collection)*	1 2 3 4 5
Field Notes	
A. Rich descriptions with a scope and depth of detail that put the reader into the setting	
B. Descriptions are objective and opinion-free	
C. Word choices in descriptions have neutral connotations	
Assessments	
D. Evidence of appropriate choice of assessment	
E. Assessments administered accurately	
F. Responses recorded clearly with observations noted	
Transcripts	
G. Accurately and clearly transcribed	
H. Complete	
2. *Transformational Knowledge*	1 2 3 4 5
A. Field notes and transcripts coded and summarized	
B. Codes are reasonable and "fall out" of the data	
C. Assessments accurately scored and summarized in tables or graphs	
3. *Explanatory Knowledge*	1 2 3 4 5
A. Conclusions and interpretations are contextual rather than emotional	
B. Examples from data sources adequately support conclusions and interpretations	
C. Conclusions and interpretations include statements that encompass the depth and breadth of constructs being analyzed	
D. Conclusions and interpretations are situated within the scope of the data, close to the data"	
4. *Extending Knowledge*	2 3 4 5
A. Construct is considered from multiple perspectives beyond the data sources	
B. Evaluative statements are connected to reflective process	
C. Goals and questions are derived from evaluative statements	

The goal of the course is to help candidates learn to reflect on student learning to guide instructional decision-making. Each semester candidates learn to follow the teaching model well, in terms of using the parts of the lesson format and administering various prepared assessments. They usually bond easily with the children, getting to know their interests and how secure they are with literacy tasks.

The most difficult part of the course is the heart of Clay's instructional method – the teacher/student interactions which determine the teacher's instructional moves. In other words, candidates must learn to reflect – collect, analyze, and interpret data and use the information to make moment-by-moment instructional decisions. This has always been a challenge for undergraduates.

The reflective part of the course has undergone multiple revisions over the years. A reflective journal was always part of the course requirements. The earlier versions usually included reflection on the student's learning and reflection on the candidate's teaching practices. Often candidates were given two questions to answer: What did you learn about your child? What did you learn about your own teaching?

EARLY RESULTS WITH REFLECTION JOURNALS

Content analysis of journals from 2004 revealed the limitations of the entries. Here are some typical responses in categories:

- Comments on the children's behavior

    "Joshua would not sit down to work today."
    "Joey was very good today. He did everything I asked him to do."
    "He was very distracted today. The teacher said he didn't have his medicine."
    "She loved the story I read to her."

- General statements about children's skills

    "Sara can't read very well."
    "He can't remember to point to words. I have to keep telling him."
    "Letter writing is hard for him."
    "She has problems with phonics."
    "He has trouble sounding out words."
    "I can see that my child is going to be a great reader."

- General statements about teacher's actions

    "I need to work on my prompts."
    "I said 'good job' too much."

None of the above would lead directly to instructional actions. They were not strong reflective statements. Some statements, such as "Josh would not sit down to work today" lacked detail and focus on instruction. What was the task? What direction was given? Was he excited about something?

Others, such as, "she has problems with phonics" or "he has trouble sounding out words" or "letter writing is hard" are vague general statements. Again, what data was collected to reach these conclusions? What part of the process was hard? What exactly was the child doing? What strategies did s/he try?

Over the years, many different strategies were tried in the course to help candidates grow as reflective practitioners. One of the first tactics was to require candidates to audiotape lessons, listen to them, and write field notes from the lessons. The reflection journal was to be used to think about the field notes and interpret them. Both the field notes and the reflections were submitted for evaluation, sometimes as a double entry journal. The results were similar to the responses cited above. Field notes tended to be speculations or conclusions rather than actual data collection, and so, reflections were limited as in earlier examples.

Use of Transcription

The next phase included transcription of audio or video tapes or section of tapes. The rationale was that transcription would slow the process down and make the interactions easier to analyze. The candidates were taught to transcribe and then code the transcripts, looking for evidence of early literacy concepts and principles. This process was modeled repeatedly in class, and candidates had opportunities to share their analyses with the instructor and peers. Reflections were written from the transcripts analyses.

When candidates were supported to collect data in a clearly defined process and helped to analyze the data, some findings were as follows:

1. Candidates carefully transcribed their lessons and were able to code types of teacher and student actions. For example, they would identify when the child was doing "word work" (Clay, 2005) and what particular strategies the child was using. (Word work is what the child does when he is using multiple strategies to decode a word.) They would notice book talk (talking about the book), prompting, probing, and reinforcing by the tutor.

2. Candidates then often wrote reflections without reference to the evidence of the transcription. In other words, the reflection was about something other than what was noted in their transcripts. One student wrote extensive field notes about the child's "word work," and then wrote a reflection about

how she finished her lessons sooner than the other teacher candidates. The data collected was seen as complete in itself and not part of the reflection process.

3. Some candidates wrote general statements in their reflections that were based on limited or atypical evidence. "My child is phonemically aware because he knew the sound of 't'." (This probably reflects lack of knowledge of the task. Phonemic awareness and letter/sound correspondences are not the same thing, and certainly one example is not enough for such a generalization.)

4. The transcripts included examples of misinformation, based on limited knowledge of spelling conventions, which were usually not noted in the reflections. "All the vowels in 'favorite' are silent." (This candidates' explicit knowledge of content was lacking.)

A few candidates were able to use the process fairly well. An example of a *useful* reflective statement follows:

When Jamie read, "The man fell down the hop," instead of "hole," I should have noticed that it didn't make sense. I probably should have asked the student, "Does that make sense?" instead of having the child immediately try to sound out the word.

In this example, the candidate used a specific situation – data coded in a transcript – and reflected on what it meant and what could have happened instead. This type of reflective thinking can lead to change in practice.

In most of the above examples, the reflection rubric had not come into use yet. Once the rubric was created and used to guide candidates' reflective work, progress was made.

USE OF THE REFLECTION RUBRIC

In the current version of the literacy course, the reflection rubric is used to guide candidates' reflection on interactions with children in the clinical setting. The four steps on the rubric are discussed and practiced separately and as a whole while the candidates tutor first or second graders. There are currently four separate but related applications of the process in the course: administering assessments, daily lesson planning, moment by moment teacher/student interactions, and summaries of learning.

Using the Reflection Process with Assessments

As they tutor, candidates collect different forms of data, beginning with prepared assessment protocols, such as a version of concepts of print assessment, phonemic awareness tasks, and running records of books students read. These prepared assessment protocols require the teacher candidate to follow the instructions carefully and record answers faithfully.

Later in the course, candidates create their own assessments, specific to the students, evaluate products, and review transcripts. Through this experience, candidates learn to use assessments common to early literacy as well as analyzing children's products day to day. Each time the emphasis is on formative assessment. The data is analyzed and interpreted and used to inform the next steps in instruction.

As each type of assessment data is collected, candidates complete a "Knowledge Construction Sheet," a guide that prompts them to assemble the data, analyze it, interpret it, and extend the knowledge. Table 7.2 is a Knowledge Construction Sheet submitted by a teacher candidate for feedback. The assessment was a teacher-made sight word inventory. Words were taken from familiar books that the student had read several times over the course of 4-5 weeks. Words were presented in isolation on cards, and the student sorted them into words known and words not known. This was not a teaching tool, but a way to assess what words the student had acquired through reading.

The teacher candidate attached the data and analysis table to the Knowledge Construction Sheet – a list with fifty-five words with check marks for those known. The analysis was simply counting the number known and making a summary table. Candidates were encouraged to make interpretive statements that clearly connect with the data from the assessment.

Sara interpreted the results from this assessment and set a goal based on the results, "continue to build sight vocabulary through repeated reading." Then she made a connection to theory. Later examples will show how Sara pulled information from several such assessments into a summary of learning for her student.

Using the Reflection Process in Day to Day Lesson Planning

In addition to assessment protocols, which include the four steps from the reflection rubric, candidates learn to write observation notes in their lesson plan forms. The lesson plan form includes space for notes and requires interpretive statements at the end of the plan. The next day's plan should include a goal or outcome that follows from the previous day's interpretive statements. See Table 7.3 for an example.

Table 7.2: Results of an Individual Assessment

Knowledge Construction Sheet

Date: 11/3/10 Teacher Candidate: Sara

Focus for data collection: student Sight Vocabulary

1. *Type of Data Collected (attached):*
_____ *Transcript (what section of lesson)*
_____ *Field notes*
__X_ *Assessment (what assessment?)* Teacher vocabulary list to sort, made from three familiar books
_____ *Product analysis (what product)*:

2. *Transformation (analysis attached)* Teacher-made protocol and summary

3. *Interpretive statements:*
1. Student recognized 40 of the 55 words on the list. (73%)
2. Student realized the words were from his books and looked them up on his own.

4. *Extension*
Goals: Continue to build sight vocabulary through repeated reading.
Theory connections: According to Clay, students can commit words to memory by examining them in different contexts, including writing them or building them with letter magnets.

In the sample in Table 7.3 Sara had set two outcomes for the student. In writing, she hoped he would stretch words, pop up fingers as he heard sounds in the word, draw boxes for the number of sounds, and put appropriate letters in the boxes to match the sounds.

In reading, Sara wanted Andy to track words – run his finger under a troublesome word while saying the word slowly. The idea is that the student will attend to the letters in the word and match them to the sounds he is speaking.

In her notes, Sara said he tracked some words in the familiar book readings (section #3). In guided writing (section #4), she noted that he was reluctant to use the popping technique while writing, but did it freely while walking outside.

In the last section (section #6), Sara decides to continue to work on these sound/symbol techniques, perhaps starting where he is comfortable with individual words that he does not have to write. The next day's plan starts with a continuation of the target outcomes.

After the first few weeks of classes in which the reflection process was introduced, Sara's lesson plans began to show continuity. Outcomes were used to guide note-taking. Notes were summarized and new outcomes of goals were set for the next day. In her final summation in Table 7.4, Sara mentions the flow of her lessons.

Table 7.3: Reading Buddies Tutoring Plan

Child's Name: Andy *Date:* 10/13/2010

1. Goal for tutor or outcome for student: Pop fingers for writing; track words while reading

2. Familiar Books: Notes:
Mrs. Wishy Washy tracked some words
Just like me

3. Running Record Book: The Present
RUNNING RECORD NOT INCLUDED IN THE TABLE
 # words in the book: 30 *# errors:* 2 *Accuracy rate:* 93%
Self-Correction rate: 1/3
Strategies observed: finger pointing, picture cues, using islands of certainty, monitoring for meaning, rereading, skipping a word and then returning, guessing and then tracking to check, starting to say a word, recognizing familiar parts of words, cross-checking

4. Guided Writing
Text written: Spiderman sprays out his web. (Shaded words and letter "w" were written by student without assistance.)
Notes:
Reluctant to pop fingers/attempt unknown word.
Took the pencil from me to write "cut."
Watched me pop fingers and draw boxes for "web." Helped with 'w'.
Outside on the way to meet his mom, he stretched words and pooped fingers unassisted.
He spelled other words – apple, tree.

5. New Book Yippy Day, Yippy Doo
Notes:
Took book out of my hand and read it.
When he missed a word, he went back and tracked it without prompting.
Made a connection between Yippy Doo and Scooby Doo.

6. Questions, new goals or outcomes, new or continuing direction
Continue to work on popping fingers for sounds in words until he is comfortable doing it in a sentence writing.
Maybe pick some separate words and have him stretch them like he did outside, then make boxes.
Gradually work up to sentences.

Using the Reflection Process in Moment by Moment Teacher/Student Interactions

In the tutoring situation, the teacher candidate must also develop skill in minute-by-minute decision making based on the same knowledge construction process. One strategy still used in the course is transcription of parts of the lesson plans. Candidates audio or videotape their lessons with the students. They are required to transcribe a section periodically, for example, a new book introduction and reading or a guided writing session.

Once the transcription is completed (the data is collected and prepared for analysis), the candidates code the transcript for teacher/student interactions. They use categories such as: prompting for strategies, probing, reinforcement, book talk. These codes come from their course readings.

Once interactions have been coded, candidates analyze each code set for effectiveness of the interaction. Again, they use the knowledge construction guide to support this process. Once during the middle of the semester, each candidate meets with the instructor to watch a videotape of a lesson. At this time, the instructor can scaffold the process by pointing out positive features of the lesson and areas for improvement.

On her Knowledge Construction Sheet, Sara:

- made careful transcriptions (data collection);
- coded them and created tables of the coded items and how often they appeared (transformation);
- wrote interpretive statements such as: I engaged in talk about the writing topic 11 times, gave 6 reinforcements;
- wrote a goal to give more specific reinforcements.

In this product, Sara does not analyze the data as completely as possible, for example, she did not analyze the "writing topic talk" or the "reinforcements" further. When she sets a goal for "more specific reinforcements," there is no evidence to provide support for her statement.

Using the Reflection Process in Summative Products

The final products for the course are summaries of what candidates have learned about their students and about themselves. Again, they start by compiling and organizing data – putting together all the assessment information they have, including notes on lesson plans. This creates a data file that will provide evidence for their interpretive statements. Then they analyze the data, cutting across the data types looking for similar information from different sources, make interpretive statements, and set goals of a summative nature.

In the student section, candidates write about many basic literacy skills. One category is "sight vocabulary." Sara wrote about her student's sight vocabulary:

- Andy has a large sight vocabulary. Evidence for this statement:

    1. On the initial sight word list at the beginning of the semester, Andy recognized 11 of 20 on the pre-primer list.

Helping Teacher Candidates Develop the Skills of Reflective Practitioners 123

2. When reviewing sight word cards (Nov. 3) that were constructed from his familiar books, Andy recognized 40 of 55 words (73 percent), including 2 of the 9 words he had missed on the earlier pre-primer list.
3. On an IRI at the end of the semester, Andy scored

- 17 out of 20 on pre-primer,
- 17 out of 20 on the primer,
- 15 out of 20 on the first grade, and
- 7 out of 20 on the second grade list.

This summation shows the effect of a focus on data collection, analysis, interpretation, and extension. The summation of the student's skill level at the point at which it was compiled is based on solid data collected and carefully analyzed. Data from several different sources was used to triangulate the interpretive statement.

The other final product for the course is a summary of candidate learning. Candidates gather data related to their own knowledge and skills as teachers in early literacy. Sara's summation can be found Table 7.4. She is clearly reflecting on her own practice, citing evidence (which is not included in this chapter), and setting goals for herself as she moves forward. There is still work to be done, but the difference between this summary reflection and the earlier reflections is quite striking.

This example was typical of the class responses. While certainly still limited by lack of experience, these junior level candidates seem to be moving in the right direction towards building a reflective practitioner stance.

CONCLUSION

This chapter shows examples of teacher candidates working with a Reflection Rubric which guides their use of a process for reflection on learning. The four parts of the process presented helped candidates become more deliberate in reflection.

Building this rubric has effectively created a definition of "reflection" as a research process – collect, analyze, interpret, and act on data. This definition changes reflection on practice from an open-ended nebulous essay to a process grounded in data collection and analysis, a process that leads to stronger, more defensible instructional decisions.

The rubric was originally designed to support seniors who developed research questions and completed action research projects in their student teaching placements. At first, this was a daunting task for the seniors. Con-

Table 7.4: Summary Reflections on Practice

Use of the Lesson Format
During the majority of tutoring sessions I used all of the sections of Marie Clay's lesson format. The exceptions occurred on days that assessments were completed in place of the writing portion of the lesson. On most days we read familiar books, read the running record book, introduced a new book, and then completed the writing portion.
The writing portion was difficult for me to do at the beginning, but it got easier as both Andy and I got more comfortable with it. I still could use some practice on popping the word to break the sounds apart in a word.

Reinforcements
During the reading and writing sessions with Andy I tried to use specific reinforcements about Andy's reading and writing strategies. For example on page 63 I used a specific reinforcement to tell Andy I liked the way that he used the first letter or sound to figure out the word. More evidence of this can be found on page 59 when I told Andy that it was great that he knew there was a vowel there, but that it was an I and not an E. I need to work on providing more reinforcements during the course of the lesson.

Book talk
If Andy did not, I initiated book talk with every new book and with the majority of familiar books and running record books. The majority of the time, I was successful in engaging Andy in book talk. We talked about what the characters were doing or how they related to him. Evidence of this can be found in a new book transcript on page 63 where I initiated book talk about the characters in *Just Like Me*. From this book talk, I discovered that Andy understood which character the text was referring to.

Prompting for Strategies
I prompted Andy to use tracking and chunking as reading strategies. Tracking the words was the most successful prompt. This prompt most often helped Andy to avoid omitting or adding words and to make sure that all of the letters fit the word, not just the first few.
Although I was consistent with the tracking prompt, I could have modeled the chunking prompt more so that Andy would be able to use it on his own. I only modeled it a few times and I never observed Andy doing it alone.

Phonemic Awareness
Although I dealt with issues relating to phonemic awareness this semester, I believe that my phonemic awareness has improved. Initially I often had trouble pulling the word apart while we were popping fingers. In the beginning I had to pause for a few moments and think before doing it with Andy. I also had to be extremely conscious of how I was pronouncing sounds and that I was not adding an /uh/ sound. Towards the end of the semester, I noticed during the last week it was becoming easier to pop fingers and that I was requiring less time to think about the task. While assessing Andy's ability to blend sounds, I struggled on some of the longer words to say each sound without blending them together.

> **The Reflection Process**
> The lessons that I completed with Andy typically involved all of the aspects of Marie Clay's lesson plan format. During each portion of the lessons, I recorded notes about Andy's performance. For example, during familiar books, I kept a record of what Andy struggled with and what strategies he was implementing. After we were finished with the familiar books I would address the issue with Andy and during the next lesson observe to see if Andy had corrected the issue during the next reading of the book.
> I also recorded notes of what Andy said and did during the writing portion of the lesson. For example, on page 102, I wrote that Andy said he didn't know if it was an S or a Z so he would just write both (highlighted in orange).
> The learner outcome influenced what I observed or what I did with Andy that day. On the days that the goal was to track while reading, I observed Andy's reading closely and recorded when he tracked, and if he did not do so, I would prompt. I also used the sentences we made during the writing session to practice tracking.
> From the notes that I made during the lesson or notes that I recorded after the lesson I attempted to make new goals to extend the current goal or to begin focusing our attention on something new. For example, once I was comfortable with Andy's tracking progress, I changed the goal to popping fingers successfully since I had noted on previous lessons that he was not successful with it yet.

vinced of the importance of the research, faculty began moving parts of the process into earlier classes, which has helped to develop a new understanding of the universality of the research process in teaching and learning. Currently, candidates are learning to teach the process to children.

The importance of the reflective practitioner cannot be overstated in education today. Defining the process as research has opened up many opportunities to provide specific instruction in discrete aspects of the process, and is providing candidates with tools to become agents of change as they move out into the schools and classrooms of their own.

REFERENCES

Clay, M.M. (2005). *Literacy lessons designed for individuals: Part two, teaching procedures.* Portsmouth, NH: Heinemann.
Dewey, J. (1933). *How we think.* Lexington, MA: C.C. Heath. (Original work published 1901.)
Roskos, K. Vukelich, C. & Risko, V. (2001). Reflection and learning to teach reading: A critical review of literacy and general teacher education studies. *Journal of Literacy Research, 3*(4), 595-635.
Schon, D. (1987). *Educating the reflective practitioner.* San Francisco, CA: Jossey-Bass.

Closing

I tell my candidates to always provide a closing for each lesson they teach, so I certainly don't want to close this book with simply "The End." Closure is meant to briefly review what the content was about, what was important about it, and how it can be used. Closure can also add that one additional piece of information that might make all the difference.

What was this book about? It was about the need for change agents in the classroom and how college and university teachers might prepare their candidates to take on this role. The important theme is that the constructivist paradigm can be instrumental in teaching candidates how to learn and how to teach; thus providing them a model for change agency. The practical applications of constructivist teaching included in each chapter can be used to influence candidates' own learning as well as the learning of their future students.

One additional thought is this: The authors of this book hope that you will recall Turning Points in your own learning and in the teaching of your candidates. Tell your stories to your students. Use them for reflection, encouragement, and motivation to continue on. That's what we're all about, learning from each other and teaching from the heart.

Contributors

About the Contributors

Jill E. Cole, Ed. D. is Associate Professor of Education at Wesley College and serves as the Program Chair for Education K-8. Previously, she taught elementary and middle school for 24 years.

Paula P. Daniels, M.Ed. is a first grade teacher in the Smyrna School District with five years of experience teaching first grade and four years of experience teaching third grade. She is also certified for Special Education.

Marcia P. Lawton, Ph.D. is Professor of Education at Wesley College. Previously she taught special education for 10 years, literacy methods and special education courses at Delaware State University and the University of Delaware, and worked with teachers to develop clinical methods for Title I reading programs.

Leah T. Lembo, Ph.D. is currently Director of Student Teaching and Visiting Assistant Professor of Curriculum and Instruction at Skidmore College. Previously, she taught as a classroom teacher and art specialist for 16 years.

Ivey Mask is a graduate student at Wesley College.

B. Patricia Patterson, Ed.D is currently Professor of Education and Director of Graduate Studies at Wesley College. She presents nationally and internationally, often at Science Educators' Research Association conferences.

Patti L. Sandy, M.Ed. has been a teacher for 33 years. She is a National Board Certified Teacher at Campus Community School, where she teachers first grade. She has also taught preschool.

Megan Stoffa is a teacher candidate in her junior year at Wesley College.

Kristin Thompson, M.Ed. is a 2nd/3rd grade teacher at Campus Community School. She has been teaching six years.

Jamie Whitman-Smithe, Ph.D. is Associate Professor of Education at Wesley College. Previously, she taught middle school and in a school for persons with disabilities.

www.ingramcontent.com/pod-product-compliance
Lightning Source LLC
Chambersburg PA
CBHW021852300426
44115CB00005B/125